Whistler and his Circle

15 *Nocturne: Palaces*, 1879-80

WHISTLER

AND HIS CIRCLE

———

ETCHINGS AND LITHOGRAPHS
FROM THE
COLLECTION OF THE ART GALLERY OF ONTARIO

———

Katharine A. Lochnan

ORGANIZED AND CIRCULATED
BY THE ART GALLERY OF ONTARIO

ITINERARY

Kitchener/Waterloo Art Gallery, Kitchener
4 September – 12 October, 1986

Chatham Cultural Centre, Chatham
5 December – 28 December, 1986

The Art Gallery of Peterborough, Peterborough
4 March – 29 March 1987

Art Gallery of Northumberland, Cobourg
24 April – 24 May, 1987

Cover:
23 *Nocturne: The River at Battersea*, 1878 (detail)

The Art Gallery of Ontario is generously funded by the
Province of Ontario, Ministry of Citizenship and Culture.

Financial support for the Gallery's operation is also
received from the Municipality of Metropolitan Toronto
and the Government of Canada through the Museums
Assistance Programme of the National Museums of
Canada, and the Canada Council.

Canadian Cataloguing in Publication Data

Art Gallery of Ontario
  James McNeill Whistler and his Circle

Catalogue of an exhibition held at the Kitchener/
Waterloo Art Gallery, Sept. 12-Oct. 12, 1986 and
other museums.
ISBN 0-919777-36-8

1. Whistler, James McNeill, 1834-1903 — Exhibitions.
2. Art Gallery of Ontario. I. Whistler, James
McNeill, 1834-1903. II. Lochnan, Katharine A.
(Katharine Aileen), 1946-   . III. Kitchener-
Waterloo Art Gallery. IV. Title.

NE2012.W45A4 1986   769.92′4   C86-094473-5

To Esther Gelber (1917–1983),
whose refined sensibility found a natural expression
in the superb Whistlers which she presented
to the Gallery.

27 *Draped Figure Reclining*, c. 1893

IN 1984 the Art Gallery of Ontario and the Metropolitan Museum of Art in New York mounted the largest exhibition of Whistler's etchings to take place since the memorial exhibitions that followed his death in 1903. This was the culmination of many years of research by our Curator of Prints and Drawings, Dr. Katharine Lochnan, and was very well received internationally.

The scale of the exhibition, and the light-sensitivity of the works themselves, made wider circulation impossible. Fortunately, the Gallery has been building up its own Whistler holdings for the past decade, and now has the largest group in a public collection in Canada. This has enabled us to mount an exhibition that contains many rare and fine impressions of the artist's etchings and lithographs.

It is interesting to note that the first Whistler etchings to enter the collection came from Sir Edmund Walker, the founder of the Gallery, and a Canadian pioneer print collector. Other early gifts came from the painter Edmund Morris and the friends of C.V. Blake. Some of these impressions were shown in the first, and probably the largest, print show ever to take place in Toronto, the *Black and White* exhibition of over a thousand works, mounted by the Art Museum of Toronto (now the Art Gallery of Ontario) in 1912. A number were given by the Canadian National Exhibition, which held important art exhibitions in Toronto earlier in this century.

Recent additions to this collection have been made possible by generous gifts from private and corporate doners. We are extremely grateful to Touche Ross and Co.; the Trier Fodor Foundation; Mrs. Peter Maclachlan; the Canadian Imperial Bank of Commerce; the Dorothy Isabella Webb Trust; Mr. and Mrs. Ralph Presgrave; Inco Limited; Mr. Jim Dickinson; Mr. and Mrs. Arthur Gelber; Norcen Energy Resources Limited; and the late Mrs. Dora Mavor Moore and Anna Hoyt Mavor.

We hope that the exhibition will give great pleasure to those who live in outlying parts of the Province of Ontario, especially to those who were unable to visit the Gallery to see the Whistler etchings exhibition in 1984.

William J. Withrow
Director
Art Gallery of Ontario

13 *Nocturne*, 1879-80

ACKNOWLEDGEMENTS

IT may seem rather soon after *The Etchings of James McNeill Whistler*, mounted in 1984, for another Whistler exhibition to appear at the Art Gallery of Ontario. While the first publication focused on the sources and evolution of Whistler's etching style, and included only the finest impressions from British, American and Canadian collections, this exhibition is drawn from our own holdings, and concentrates on Whistler's influence: the other end of the spectrum.

I wanted to catalogue the Whistler holdings of the Art Gallery of Ontario, which have been built piece by piece during the past decade, and to explore the Whistler inheritance. This subject has already been examined by Allen Staley, editor of the exhibition catalogue *From Realism to Symbolism: Whistler and His World* (New York: Columbia University, 1971), and by Robert Getscher, in *The Stamp of Whistler* (Oberlin: Allen Memorial Art Museum, 1977). It is not my intention here, limited as I am by the scope and content of a modest collection, to do more than add a postscript to their work.

I have tried to look at the Whistler circle largely through letters and memoirs, in an attempt to clarify Whistler's attitude to art education, and to his so-called "pupils" and "followers." Wherever possible, I have let the *dramatis personae* speak for themselves. They provide the best insight into the dynamic of the Whistler circle, one which was at the same time artistically stimulating and a political hornet's nest.

We could never have built this collection without the welcome support of private and corporate donors. It is to them, and to the late Esther Gelber in particular, that I would like to dedicate this work. Although we have begun to collect late in the day, the highlights of this exhibition, which contains several rare and unique impressions, is a tribute to Toronto philanthropists.

I would also like to thank the friends and colleagues who have helped me complete this manuscript: David Kiehl, Associate Curator in the Department of Prints and Photographs at the Metropolitan Museum of Art, who checked a number of the *catalogue raisonné* references unavailable in Toronto; Rosemarie L. Tovell, Curator of Canadian Prints and Drawings at the National Gallery of Canada, who provided biographical information about the Canadians in the exhibition; Glenda Milrod, Head of Extension Services, Art Gallery of Ontario, who encouraged me to organize the exhibition; my Assistant, Brenda Rix, who made it possible for me to get away to write; my Secretary, Catherine Garside, who assembled the photographs and patiently incorporated the seemingly endless corrections to the manuscript; Robert Stacey, who edited the manuscript with great care, and Richard Male, who has designed and produced yet another beautiful catalogue.

I would also like to thank my husband, George Yost, for his support of the work in progress.

Katharine A. Lochnan
Curator of Prints and Drawings

fig. 1, Adolphe Rajon (French, 1843-1888), *Portrait of Whistler*
Lithograph, 29.2 x 21.6 cm (sheet), Gift of Touche Ross, 1979, Acc. no. 79/210

JAMES McNEILL WHISTLER (1834-1903) was an undisciplined art student. From the time he arrived in Paris from the United States of America in 1855, he played truant from Gleyre's Academy, preferring to learn his craft in the Louvre and find his subjects in the streets of the Left Bank.

It was in this artistic bohemia that he set out to free himself from the constraints imposed by his puritanical mother, and threw himself into a career and a social life which, if it had its ups and downs, was never dull. He became a master of "*blague*," a philosophy of life which involved "the passing over of vexations with a glorious carelessness."[1] What began as a carefree exaltation of his considerable artistic talents was later adapted as a strategy for self-defence.

Whistler was gregarious by nature; he loved an audience, and hated being alone. With his sense of style, good looks, generous nature, charm and ready wit, he was always able to attract others to him. He associated initially with the "English Group" in Paris, which included Edward J. Poynter, L.M. Lamont, George Du Maurier and Thomas Armstrong (see fig. 2), with whom he had nothing in common artistically. Lamont and Armstrong later wrote memoirs which, together with Du Maurier's correspondence, provide some of our earliest insights into Whistler's character and development.

In the autumn of 1858 he fell in with two young French artists, Henri Fantin-Latour (1836-1904) and Alphonse Legros (1837-1911), who looked to the Realist painter Gustave Courbet (1817-1877) for leadership. Courbet flew in the face of convention: he did not believe in schools or in the master-pupil relationship, and did not see himself playing the role of teacher. Petitioned by a group of dissatisfied students from the Ecole des Beaux-Arts to open a school, Courbet wrote to the paper *Courrier du dimanche*, "I do not have, I cannot have, pupils. I, who believe that every artist should be his own teacher, cannot dream of setting myself up as a professor."[2] He would have encouraged the three young artists to look for their subjects in modern life, and paint what they found in nature. His 1855 "Manifesto" was his credo and provided them with a set of guidelines.

For six months in 1861-62, Courbet did run a school. He promoted his idea that "every artist should be his own teacher," and that "art is completely individual" and is based on talent and the study of tradition.[3] Fantin-Latour was one of his students. While Whistler does not appear to have attended the school, Courbet's maxims by this time formed the basis of his own. In 1865, when he painted with Courbet at Trouville, Courbet considered him his "pupil."

At the outset, Whistler saw Legros (fig. 2) and Fantin as his peers. They called themselves the "*Société des trois*," but had little in common except a desire to create a new art based in modern life, and to assist each other in the launching of their artistic careers. After moving to London in May 1859, Whistler encouraged Fantin and Legros to follow him. Legros did so, but proximity did not draw them closer. Legros became too friendly with Whistler's brother-in-law, and rival etcher, Francis Seymour Haden (nos. 45-47).

fig. 2, Alphonse Legros (British, 1837-1911), *Portrait of Thomas Armstrong*
Pencil drawing on laid paper, 36.8 x 26.0 cm, Art Gallery of Ontario. Gift of E.R. Rolph 1935.

Haden (1818-1910) was responsible for introducing Whistler to the art of etching. A physician by profession, he was also an *amateur* whose interest focused largely on collecting fine examples of the work of Rembrandt and the seventeenth-century Dutch School. He was inspired to ply the needle creatively by the success of Whistler's "French Set" of 1858 (nos. 1-3), which was published from his home in London. As long as Haden continued to admire Whistler's work, and view him as the artist in the family, they remained on good terms. But once Haden began to see himself as an artist in his own right, and his superb Thames drypoints attracted the attention of Philippe Burty, the leading critic of etching in Paris, Whistler mounted a campaign against him, and stopped etching for seven years. He was mortified by the critical acclaim Haden received on both sides of the Channel, while his own outstanding etchings inspired only negative criticism from Burty.

In the mid-1860s, after falling in with the Pre-Raphaelite circle of Dante Gabriel Rossetti (1828-1882), and with the concept of "Art for Art's Sake" in London, Whistler went through an artistic crisis. He lamented his earlier lack of academic diligence, and threw himself into a private course of study under the tutelage of Albert Moore (1841-1893). In his correspondence with Fantin he began to campaign vigorously against Legros, suggesting at first that the *Société des trois* should consist of the two of them, and then that Moore replace Legros. In May 1867, having gone through an aesthetic about–face from Realism to Aestheticism, Whistler lamented the fact that he had not been a pupil of Ingres, and cut himself off from the first generation of his artistic acquaintances: he denounced Courbet's Realism, ceased to correspond with Fantin, and dispatched Seymour Haden through the plate-glass window of a Paris restaurant. The brothers-in-law never spoke again. Three years later, in 1870, Whistler distanced himself from Albert Moore, fearing that his close imitations might be taken for the work of Moore himself.

By 1870 the Paris art scene had changed considerably. Edouard Manet (1832-1883) had succeeded Courbet as the leader of the Realist movement, and both he and Edgar Degas (1834-1917) were formidable rivals of Whistler's. As Fantin gravitated toward Manet, Whistler pulled back, and the close bond of loyalty between them was broken. Whistler adopted a fiercely independent stance which he retained for the rest of his life. He never became part of a group. When Degas, an old friend from his student days, wrote to invite him to contribute to the first Impressionist exhibition, Whistler neglected to answer his letter. Unfortunately, the decision to remove himself from the competitive Paris art scene led to a diminution of his talents.

Whistler began instead to cultivate his own following. He surrounded himself with young artists who admired his Thames etchings of 1859 (no. 5): these included Percy Thomas, the son of Whistler's patron and dealer Serjeant Ralph Thomas, and Matthew White Ridley (1837-1888) (no. 56). Through Ridley, Whistler was introduced to the lawyer, Edwin Edwards (no. 48). Whistler preferred to see himself as a mentor, advising his circle of friends on etching, and criticising the results.

The first real Whistler "followers" were the brothers Walter and Harvey Greaves, the sons of a Chelsea boat-builder who lived a few doors from Whistler's house on Lindsay Row, now Cheyne Walk (fig. 3). In return for being his "devoted slaves," Whistler was "charming" to them and flattered them, saying, "you are the pride of one end of the row, and I am the pride of the other."[4] The basis of the relationship lay in an exchange of services: the Greaves acted as Whistler's studio assistants, and at night rowed him on the Thames, where he conceived his "nocturnes." In return, Whistler taught them to draw and paint, urging them to abandon the naïve style they had learnt by decorating boats, and encouraging them to imitate his own. They attended a Chelsea life drawing class together, always arriving late with Whistler in the fore. While he worked directly from the model, the Greaves would sit on either side and copy Whistler's drawing.

Walter Greaves (1846-1930) was the better artist of the two, and complied absolutely with Whistler's wishes. He slavishly copied Whistler's manners, dress and Thames views to such effect that he almost lost his identity.[5] Having encouraged this tendency, Whistler then became irritated by it, and warned the Greaves in a letter written in the early 1870s not to imitate him too closely: "you know how I continually invent – and invention you know is the cream of the whole affair and so easy to destroy the freshness of it."[6]

Whistler produced some of his best work during the first twenty years of his career, from 1859-79. Unfortunately, success went to his head, and he began to take liberties with a trusting patron, the Liverpool shipping magnate Frederick Leyland. When asked to perform some modest alterations to Leyland's newly decorated dining room at Prince's Gate in London, Whistler completely transformed it into the "Peacock Room" without Leyland's permission. Incensed more by Whistler's "indiscretions" with his wife than by the unauthorized destruction of his dining room, Leyland refused to pay him. While the controversy was in full swing, in July 1877, the leading art critic of the age,

John Ruskin (1819-1900), attacked Whistler's integrity as a painter in *Fors Clavigera*, accusing him of "flinging a pot of paint in the public's face."[7] In desperate financial straits, and unable to sell his paintings, Whistler was forced to sue Ruskin for libel.

His work was now the centre of public attention, and the artist, adopting a *blague* stance, appeared to revel in it. The witness stand at the Ruskin court case was transformed into a stage from which Whistler could trumpet his ideas on art, which were reported daily in the press. He set out to capture the public imagination, and teach by entertaining. He intended to make Ruskin look ridiculous, to undermine his credibility and that of art critics in general. By winning the case Whistler did Ruskin irreparable damage, while he achieved international prominence. He suspended the farthing awarded in damages from his watch fob and wore it for the rest of his life. Whistler was, however, instructed to pay costs. Having just built the White House on Tite Street in Chelsea, which included an *atelier* for pupils, he had run out of credit. In May 1879 he was declared bankrupt. Bills were pasted to the exterior walls, the house was occupied by bailiffs, and its contents itemized for auction.

Although Whistler turned the occupation into high drama, conscripting the bailiffs to act as liveried waiters at his dinner table, and sending in the Greaves brothers to smuggle supplies of fine paper out of his studio, he was destined to lose all the worldly

fig. 3, James Hedderley (British, c.1815-1885), Lindsay Houses seen from the River. The Greaves' house is at the left end of the row, and Whistler's at the right. Photograph, Royal Borough of Kensington and Chelsea Libraries and Art Service.

possessions that he had assembled with such care over the years. Everything was to go on the block: his blue-and-white china, Japanese prints, kimonos, Chinese furniture, paintings and copper plates from his studio, as well as pots and pans from his kitchen. Worst of all, his beautiful White House was to be sold for a fraction of its cost to the art critic from the *Times*.

Whistler was then forty-five years of age. Despite the bravado stance he affected in public, he was a sensitive individual, and must have suffered terribly. Fortunately, the Fine Art Society intervened and commissioned him to go to Venice in September 1879 to make a series of twelve etchings, to be published in December (nos. 13-16). Much to the irritation of the directors, he played truant for almost a year. Having overshot the December deadline, he stayed on through the summer and autumn of 1880.

His winter in Venice was not an easy one. He was desperate to recoup his financial losses, and worked hard on etchings, pastels and paintings. He and his common-law wife, Maud Franklin, spent much of the winter in great discomfort: the weather was viciously cold and did irreparable damage to her health. Finally summer came, and Whistler would sit in front of Florian's or Quadri's in the Piazza San Marco, listening to the orchestras, and taking in the beauty of the place.

Early in the summer of 1880, a group of American art students, led by an American of German descent, Frank Duveneck (1848-1919), arrived in Venice. They knew of Whistler's work, and were thrilled to meet him. Starving for compliments, he was enormously gratified. He quickly adopted the Duveneck "Boys," and moved with some of them into the Casa Jancovitz at the end of the Riva degli Schiavoni. Whistler and Maud had a room next to Otto Bacher, who had a portable etching press. Bacher learnt a great deal by watching Whistler pull his proofs and acting as his studio assistant. He later published a valuable account of Whistler's Venetian etching technique. True to form, Whistler laid claim to Bacher, who wrote, "Whistler always spoke of me as one of his pupils – even as one of his favorite pupils. Of course it pleased me mightily, but I did not deserve such a title or value it at the time. There were many others who were known by this name, but I never knew the term to be applied except in an endearing way."[8] Whistler kept in touch with Bacher and saw a lot of him in London before the young artist returned to America in 1883.

Having regaled the Duveneck "Boys" with stories about the Ruskin case, Whistler returned to London in November 1880 in excellent spirits, ready to throw himself into the fray. He was desperately in need of assistance with the printing of fifty plates, which would enable him to select the twelve for the Fine Art Society exhibition due to open at the end of the month. He had originally hoped to use Ridley's press, no doubt with Ridley's assistance, but this plan had fallen through.

Soon after he began printing the plates, a young Australian named Mortimer Menpes (1855-1938) (no. 53) offered to help with the printing. Menpes was then studying under Sir Edward Poynter at the South Kensington Schools. Joseph Pennell (1860-1926), Whistler's biographer, wrote scathingly of how "dropping Poynter, South Kensington, and his own ambition," Menpes "hastened to throw himself at the feet of the master and inscribe himself a pupil."[9]

A year later, when the printing of the "First Venice Set" edition was more than they

fig. 4, Whistler and Mortimer Menpes.
Photograph, Library of Congress, Pennell Collection.

could handle, a talented young artist, Walter Richard Sickert (1860-1942) (no. 61) came to see Whistler. His first impressions of Whistler were of a man "Sunny, courageous, elegant, *soigné*. Entertaining, *serviable*, gracious, good-natured, easy-going. A *charmeur* and a dandy, with a passion for work."[10] Sickert was then a pupil of Alphonse Legros at the Slade School of Fine Art, London; Whistler encouraged him to bail out, saying, "You've wasted your money, Walter; there's no use wasting your time too!"[11]

Sickert and Menpes supplanted the Greaves in the post-Venice period as Whistler's "followers." They were allowed to sign themselves "pupils of Whistler," and were told Whistler's "secret of drawing," which Sickert scribbled on his shirt sleeve. They learnt something of Whistler's theory and technique by acting as studio assistants and running errands. In turn, Whistler helped to form their taste, taking them to museums to admire Canaletto and Velasquez, while conceding that Rembrandt "had his good days," and maintaining that Raphael "did not count."[12]

The "followers" grew to include Theodore Roussel (1847-1926) (no. 59) in 1885. He joined the group just as Whistler's etching "Propositions" were being finalized for publication with the "Second Venice Set." The three took up etching in the style of Whistler, observing the "Propositions" to the letter. Menpes wrote, "At this time we copied Whistler in every detail.... If we etched a plate we had to etch it exactly on Whistlerian lines. If Whistler kept his plates fair, ours were so fair that they could scarcely be seen. If he adopted economy of means, using the fewest possible lines, we became so nervous that we could scarcely touch the plate lest we should over-elaborate."[13] The results were often feeble imitations, for the reason that Whistler knew all too well, and had warned the Greaves brothers about years earlier.

Whatever else the followers did to assist Whistler paled to insignificance beside their mandatory duties as loyal and vigilant conscripts in the holy war against the "enemy." Sickert, Menpes, Roussel and the Greaves formed an artistic bodyguard round the "Master." The war was fought on many levels at once, but was primarily a literary campaign fought in the press. Whistler, who described the Bible, ever at his mother's elbow, as "that splendid mine of invective," adopted biblical vocabulary to label his world: he was the "Master," his pupils the "followers."[14] His "Propositions" have about them the ring of the tablets of the law, his *Ten O'Clock* lecture of the Sermon on the Mount. He saw himself leading the "multitude" out of aesthetic captivity. He actively fought the "enemy," particularly self-appointed art critics and established arts organizations, for the rest of his life.

At his mother's insistence, Whistler had memorized great chunks of the King James version, which helps to account for his considerable literary talents and gift for language. He knew the power of speaking in parables, and loved to confound the "multitude," tossing off pithy remarks that were the envy of Oscar Wilde. On one occasion Wilde remarked, "I wish I had said that." "You will, Oscar, you will", Whistler replied. Whistler's sayings were repeated all over London, and spread to France and North America.

In the early 1880s, Whistler's studio was full of hangers-on, all of whom had roles to play in his new career as self-publicist. Sir Rennell Rodd wrote, "We had great fun over the many correspondences and the catalogues elaborated in those days in Tite Street.... He was demoniacal in controversy and the spirit of elfin mischief was developed in him to the point of genius"[15] The followers were key to the success of his campaign; Sickert and Menpes "insisted, in season and out of season, on the excellence and importance of Whistler's work" and carried on a defence "with some obstinacy in whatever papers would put up with it."[16]

They soon began to tire of this. Sickert wrote, "it was always a grief and annoyance to those who loved and admired these rare and precious qualities in Whistler that he would so constantly leave his easel for his writing desk"[17] Later the most articulate of Whistler's critics, he felt that "The real disservice that Whistler risked doing to art was the determined effort he made to buttress up any weaknesses in the walls of his own citadel, by the promulgation of somewhat arbitrary little decrees or bulls. There was almost a risk that a whole generation would swallow these edicts with their eyes shut."[18] Whistler's activities were viewed with distaste by Degas from the other side of the Channel; he reputedly said to Sickert, who had been sent to him by Whistler, "Quel dommage qu'un peintre si fin soit doublé d'un 'humbug'."[19]

Whistler did not wish to develop a group of independent young artists who could stand on their own feet and compete with him. William Rothenstein (1872-1942) (fig. 8, no. 58), who got to know Whistler in the early 1890s, wrote in his autobiography, "How far Whistler was aware of Sickert's or of Greaves's genius is problematical; I am inclined to believe he did not wish to recognize it; at any rate, he made every use of their devotion; but he saw to it that the limelight should be focused on himself; he deemed a farthing dip good enough for his disciples."[20] He required from his friends "not only loyalty and admiration, but exclusive loyalty and admiration."[21] Whenever they showed signs of independence, Whistler would castigate them; they lived in con-

"a symphony"

fig. 5, Sir Leslie Ward (British, 1851-1922), *Whistler* from *Vanity Fair* 1878
Lithograph on wove paper, 40.3 x 26.7 cm (sheet),
Gift of The Trier-Fodor Foundation, 1982, Acc. no. 82/247

stant fear of the withdrawal of his friendship, or of becoming lumped with the "enemy." In 1885, Menpes wrote to apologise for his latest indiscretion, saying, "even if I should have to sacrifice my little feelings, my interest in your work is much too genuine to allow myself to cause just one moment of trouble."[22] But when Sickert began to flex his muscles in 1885-87, and wrote to Whistler to say that he had to preserve his own independence, a cooling-off period began in their relationship.[23]

In addition to campaigning on his own behalf, Whistler set out to shake up the art societies. In 1884 he was elected a member of the moribund Society of British Artists. Two years later the Society, desperately in need of revitalization, elected him President. He ran it like an enlightened despot, packing the exhibitions with work by friends and followers, including some from the Continent. He juried member submissions severely, cutting down drastically on the number of works shown, and hanging only "on the line." This led to a furor among the old guard, and in 1888 Whistler was voted out of office. Roussel and a number of other artists resigned with him. Seeing the storm on the horizon, Menpes resigned prematurely. Whistler, who was already put out by Menpes' trip to Japan the previous year, which he felt should have been "saved" for the "Master," and by a visit of his to Seymour Haden, accused him of being "the early rat that leaves the sinking ship."[24] Menpes was nonetheless forgiven, and was present at dinner afterwards at the Hogarth Club where Whistler was in high spirits.[25]

As time went on, the followers became so deeply enmeshed in Whistler's battles that they became jealous and suspicious of each other. Sickert, like Whistler, turned against Menpes after an interview on home decoration appeared in the *Pall Mall Gazette* on 1 December 1888 in which Menpes took credit for Whistler's ideas on interior decoration. All too well aware of the immortalizing power of Whistler's pen, Sickert warned Whistler to leave Menpes "severely alone."[26] Whistler nonetheless wrote to "the kangaroo," as he called the young Australian, and told him to "blow his brains out."[27] As Menpes's star plummetted from Whistler's horizon, Sickert stepped into the limelight. A loyal follower, he decided to devote his energies to writing a "*catalogue déraisonné*" of Whistler's etchings.[28]

Whistler saw less and less of the Greaves brothers after his return from Venice, gradually losing contact with them. Supplanted and left out of his new social life, they nonetheless remained loyal and continued to paint in his style, as well as in the more naive style which they adopted whenever his back was turned. Whistler gave Sickert to believe that "the 'Greaves boys' were negligible, that what they accomplished they had from him, and that when his influence was withdrawn they relapsed into the nullity from which he had lifted them for awhile."[29] When, in the 1890s, it was brought to his attention that the brothers were still signing themselves "pupil of Whistler," he defended them, saying

They were more my pupils than anyone else has ever been – and full of talent – But, for years and years I have seen neither – so I don't know how they turned out – All my good or bad influence they may have got rid of – but certainly I shall stand by them – for at least they seem to be *loyal*…it is a dangerous thing to be a pupil of Whistler – and before now I have found that the "influence" of that curious master was of the most ephemeral kind! I really have brought up no pupil – that is I am responsible for the work of no-one – but – Walter and Harvey Greaves make an exception partly – that is to say they had *no other* master.... But again, I left them long before pupils are wont to be left.[30]

Sickert managed to remain on good terms with Whistler for a long time. Joseph Pennell acknowledged that when he met Whistler, Sickert was "a favorite pupil" and "one of his cleverest disciples."[31] Rothenstein saw him as a "famous wit," who could use a pen in a "masterly manner"; "As a talker he could hold his own with Whistler or Wilde. Further, he seemed to be on easy and familiar terms with the chief social, intellectual and political figures of the time".[32] Sickert was an attractive man, and a social and artistic rival. But Whistler did not care for rivals, and by 1893 Sickert's pen was no longer needed.

There was a long cooling-off period. When Rothenstein first met Sickert at Whistler's apartment on the rue du Bac, after Whistler moved to Paris in 1892, he noted that relations were somewhat strained: "He and Whistler were close friends, but Whistler seemed to have some grievance against him, fancied or real, and Sickert was quiet and a little constrained."[33] This undoubtedly had more to do with Sickert's exceptional abilities as an artist than any imagined disloyalty. As Rothenstein observed, "Whistler knew perfectly well who were artists to be reckoned with, and who were not."[34]

Joseph Pennell (nos. 54 and 55) soon supplanted Sickert as Whistler's most ardent and uncritical supporter. Although they had met in London some years earlier, Pennell only began to see Whistler regularly after he moved to Paris and needed help printing etchings in 1893. He knew well enough that Whistler wanted himself and his wife, Elizabeth Robins, to become "his press agents, his war correspondents, and we would not. Many before – Sickert among them – had succumbed, been squeezed dry and cast aside."[35] Despite Pennell's protestations, he and his wife were to generate numerous books and articles which are, for better or worse, the basis of Whistler studies.

Jealous of his own friendship with Whistler, Pennell was scathing about Whistler's former "followers." In the two-volume biography, *The Life of James McNeill Whistler*, which appeared in 1908, he wrote:

Whistler always had the power of attracting people to him and the devotion of one special group became almost infatuation. They were ready to do anything for him. We have heard of families estranged and of engagements and marriages broken because of him. They fought his battles; ran his errands; spied out the land for him; read his letters, when he wished it, to everybody they met. They formed a genuine little court about him. They exaggerated everything, even their devotion, and became virtually caricatures of Whistler.[36]

The followers did not take to Pennell. Rothenstein wrote, "At Whistler's I first met Joseph Pennell. I felt, the moment I met him, that he disliked me at sight.... He was so rude that when he left, Whistler was apologetic, saying: 'Never mind, Parson; you know, I always had a taste for bad company.' " Pennell remained "steadily hostile."[37] Rothenstein resented Pennell's remarks about the "followers" in the *Life* and denounced him as "an uncritical worshipper of Whistler, resentful of sharing Whistler's friendship with people who showed independence.... [H]e speaks with small respect of those whom he calls 'the followers'; yet what was he himself but one of the most sycophantic of these?"[38]

Rothenstein was a frequent visitor at the rue du Bac. Whistler, who was always interested in what he was doing and whom he was seeing, would put him at ease. Mrs. Whistler sometimes gave them tea in the studio, and Whistler would bring out his canvases. But "the priviledged occasion was not without its embarrassment; for Whistler's comments on his own work were so loving, so caressing," Rothenstein wrote, "that to find superlative expressions of praise to cap his own became…increasingly difficult and exhausting."[39]

The key to understanding Whistler's personality lies in his deep personal insecurity, a side he seldom revealed. Rothenstein caught a glimpse of that side during a memorable night visit to his studio:

We had been dining at the Hotel du Bon Lafontaine; after dinner Whistler proposed we should go to the studio.… Climbing the stairs we found the studio in darkness. Whistler lighted a single candle. He had been gay enough during dinner, but now he became very quiet and intent, as though he forgot me. Turning a canvas that faced the wall, he examined it carefully up and down, with the candle held near it, and then did the like with some others, peering closely into each. There was something tragic, almost frightening, as I stood and waited, in watching Whistler; he looked suddenly old, as he held the candle with trembling hands, and stared at his work, while our shapes threw restless, fantastic shadows, all around us. As I followed him silently down the stairs I realized that even Whistler must often have felt his heart heavy with the sense of failure.[40]

By the mid-1890s, Whistler's public reputation in Britain and France was secure: selected diatribes against the "enemy" had appeared in *The Gentle Art of Making Enemies* in 1890; *Arrangement in Grey and Black: Portrait of the Artist's Mother* entered the Luxembourg Museum, Paris, in 1891, and he received the Légion d'honneur in 1892. Whistler was vindicated. If his work was still studiously ignored by the Royal Academy in London, he was greatly admired by the promising young artists of the New English Art Club and the Glasgow School. Turning his back on the "Islanders," as he called the British, he and his wife, Beatrice Godwin, whom he had married in 1888, moved to Paris where they received friends and admirers from Britain, France and America on Sunday at their apartment on the rue du Bac. G.H. Boughton found Whistler at this time "the adored master…surrounded by the clamour of the new born babes of his 'nursery' and stifled with the thick incense of their adoration."[41]

These were Whistler's happiest years. When his wife fell ill in 1894 and died of cancer in 1896, he was desolate. Despite his public antics and the politics of the Whistler circle, there can be no question about the depth of his devotion to her. This event was the greatest crisis in his life after the Ruskin affair. It completely disoriented him and sapped his will to live. His method of coping with grief was to throw himself at once into a series of conflicts. Sickert was one of his first victims.

Sickert, who sent a heartfelt letter of sympathy, later described Beatrice's illness and death as "the brief *chemin de la Croix* that robbed him in turn of his spirit, his strength and his life."[42] However, seeing Sickert in the company of Whistler's arch-enemy, Sir

fig. 6 (also no. 38), James McNeill Whistler (American, 1834-1903), *Firelight: Joseph Pennell* 1896
W. 104, L. 152, Transfer lithograph on simile japon, 28.7 x 21.9 cm (sheet)
Gift of Touche Ross, 1978, Acc. no. 77/172

William Eden, a few months later, Whistler broke with him for good. "Though doubtless I shall miss you," he wrote, "Benedict Arnold they say, also was a pleasant desperate fellow – and our old friend of the 30 pieces, irresistible – I fancy you will have done it cheaper though poor chap!"[43]

The Pennells now became Whistler's intimates, and catered to his every whim. Although Pennell occasionally assisted with the grounding of copper plates, his services as a journalist were much more valuable. He helped to bolster the market for Whistler's lithographs: in 1894, when Pennell planned to write an article on the etchings for *Scribner's*, Whistler convinced him to write instead about the lithographs, which he was having trouble selling. After Pennell wrote the introduction to a catalogue of Whistler's lithographs in 1895, Whistler returned the compliment, writing the introduction to a catalogue of Pennell's lithographs in 1896.

The Pennells began to collect information for their biography in 1897, keeping a disjointed record of their conversations, published separately in *The Whistler Journal* in 1921. Their personal stake in the posthumous reputation of the "master" unfortunately clouded their objectivity. Whistler's desire for immortality necessitated a biographer who could be counted on to present him in the best possible light. However irritating he may have found the Pennells, they served his purpose admirably, and he chose to preserve the friendship.

Sickert, who was undoubtedly smarting over Whistler's rejection a few months earlier, and jealous of the fact that Whistler had written the introduction to Pennell's catalogue, attacked Pennell's transfer lithographs in an article in *The Saturday Review* in December 1896. He maintained that transfer lithographs, which were made by transferring drawings made on specially prepared paper to a lithographic stone, were not true lithographs. He knew well enough that to attack transfer lithography, which Whistler had been trying to validate as a medium suitable for serious artistic expression since 1887, was to attack Whistler himself.

Whistler chose to regard Sickert's comments as a veiled onslaught and induced Pennell to bring an action for libel, offering to appear as witness. He tired of the case long before it was heard. When he tried to back out, Pennell exhorted him to battle, declaring, "The case is yours as much as mine, and you must come.... Your reputation is involved. There will be an end to your lithography if we lose. You must fight."[44] Rothenstein offered his support to Sickert, aware that the action could spell financial ruin for him. Whistler, annoyed that Rothenstein was representing the "wrong side" – and forgetting that he was trying to ruin Sickert – tried to talk him out of it, saying, " 'But I have known Walter longer than you have'."[45] It was a foolish case; support for the validity of transfer lithography came not only from the keepers of the Victoria and Albert and British Museums and the master printers Way and Goulding, but from Sickert's side as well.

For Whistler, the event must have brought back heady memories of the Ruskin case. Rothenstein dined with him shortly afterward, and found him "radiant" with delight at "winning" his case. A few weeks later Rothenstein suffered the same fate as Sickert. Seeing him in Eden's presence, Whistler "put up his eye-glass, stared hard at us, and then turned his back." Rothenstein decided that "There were limits to the price one should pay for Whistler's friendship. I felt that explanation would be useless and undignified. I never saw Whistler again."[46]

In 1897-98 the International Society of Sculptors, Painters, and Gravers was founded by a group of young artists who were for the most part firm admirers of Whistler. John Lavery was Vice President, and worked harder than anyone to "help to raise a monument to Whistler by surrounding him with the best painters of the day, whose sympathy would be a proof that he was appreciated by his brethren."[47] Whistler was elected President in 1898 and ruled the society in his customary autocratic fashion. Unlike the Society of British Artists, authority rested entirely with a self-perpetuating executive, and all members were honourary. "Napoleon and I do these things," explained Whistler.[48] When he proposed that Pennell be on the executive, several members resigned in protest. The first exhibition included works by such leaders of the French *avant garde* as Bonnard, Cézanne, Degas, Manet, Monet, Redon, Renoir, and Vuillard; Boldini, Puvis de Chavannes, Klimt, and Rodin (no. 57) were listed among the honorary members.

In the autumn of 1898 Whistler founded a school in Paris to promote his ideas. It was referred to in the circular as the "Académie Whistler," but was named the Académie Carmen after one of Whistler's favourite models, who ran the operation.[49] Whistler made it clear that, while he only proposed to visit the new academy on occasion, and would have nothing to do with financial management, he planned to have everything to do with the system of teaching, and would offer his students the knowledge of a lifetime. According to Pennell,

within a few days a vast number of pupils had put their names down and expressed their intention of deserting the *ateliers* of Paris – some left the Slade and other English schools, and still others came from Germany and America. Whistler was delighted, and he told us he had heard that other *ateliers* were emptying, students coming in squads from everywhere, that the Passage was crowded, and that owners of carriages struggled with *rapins* and prize-winners to get in.[50]

Whistler saw himself carrying on the old-master tradition of teaching which was quite unlike that of Charles Gleyre (1806-1874) or Courbet. He believed that "the master should teach the pupils to draw and paint in his way, so that they should learn all he knew from him by precept and practice, and then they should either be able to help him in his work, as the pupils of the old masters did, or having learned all they could, start out and do something for themselves."[51] From the start, Whistler was a most infrequent visitor. He was very strict, forbidding talking, smoking, and drawing on the walls. He separated the men from the women, and appointed a male and female student as *massier* and *massière*. He "demanded the students to abandon all former methods of teaching unless in harmony with his own, and to approach the science as taught by himself in a simple and trustful manner."[52] His *Propositions* were framed and hung on the wall for guidance.

The students, however, were unhappy with the discipline, the vagaries of Whistler's teaching, and his prolonged absences, and left in droves. In the second year of operation, he handed over the running of the school to his *massière*, Miss Inez Bate, who had been his most successful pupil. During the third year, when he fell ill and

fig. 7 (also no. 39), James McNeill Whistler (American, 1834-1903), *Walter Sickert* 1895
W. 104, L. 152, Transfer lithograph on wove paper, 31.8 x 20.2 cm (sheet)
Gift of Touche Ross, 1978, Acc. no. 77/167

went to Corsica to recuperate, there was a mass exodus. Whistler decided to write to those who remained a "charming" letter of farewell to be read aloud by the *massière*, closing the school and bidding its pupils "God Speed."[53]

Despite the unsatisfactory nature of the experiment, Whistler maintained that the Academy Carmen was "rounded out as it should be." According to Pennell, he brooded over the prospect that

"the Walter Sickerts, the followers who, when they come after the army are called bushwhackers, crowd in and pick up what they can. No doubt Sickert promises to carry things much further than Whistler ever did, and to reveal, as it were, all the secrets, all the little things, all the last touches, Whistler held in reserve. What?"[54]

On 20 July 1899, he made Miss Bate his first apprentice. She was bound by an antiquated legal document which specified that for five years she was "not to show or sell any works without his permission, she is to help him in his work if he wants; she is to be in all things submissive while he binds himself to teach and to train her."[55] When she married a fellow-student, the American Clifford Addams (1876-1942) (no. 42), Whistler also made him an apprentice.

During Whistler's last years, the Pennells and the Bates were among those close to him. He was looked after by his wife's younger sister, Rosalind Birnie Philip, whom he had made his ward and executrix. His last years were spent in Chelsea in a house on Cheyne Walk overlooking the Thames. It was there that he died in the studio on 17 July 1903. The funeral, which took place at Old Chelsea Church, was small, and pupils and followers were conspicuous by their absence. Pennell and Menpes were among those to be found in the small crowd that gathered.[56] Whistler's coffin was draped with a purple pall on which was placed a golden laurel wreath sent by the International Society.

Following Whistler's death, there was a flurry of literary activity. The Pennells set to work at once on their *Life of James McNeill Whistler*. They contacted some of Whistler's oldest friends in hopes of reconstructing his early years, and their labours were often rewarded. In the process, they assembled the vast collection of letters and Whistleriana now in the Library of Congress, Washington. They encountered one major stumbling block: Rosalind Birnie Philip refused them access to Whistler's personal papers, disregarding the claim that they had been authorized to write the "official" biography by Whistler himself. Miss Birnie Philip ultimately gave her indispensible archive to Glasgow University Library. Within a few years, monographic memoirs were published by Bacher, Menpes, Walter and Richard Sickert, Thomas R. Way and Rothenstein, ensuring the survival not only of the facts of Whistler's life, but of the myth he had created.

Preparations began at once for the great memorial exhibitions that took place in Boston, London and Paris in 1904 and 1905, helping to spread knowledge of Whistler's work among the younger generation. They also served to stimulate collecting and inflate market values for Whistler's etchings, which reached spectacular heights before the stock market crash of 1929. The "followers" were quick to sell their rare proofs at a profit, something they would never have dared to do while Whistler was alive. The finest of these were acquired by Charles Lang Freer and other American collectors, which did much to spread a first-hand knowledge and appreciation of Whistler's work in his homeland.

A younger generation of artists from Britain, the United States and Canada flocked to Europe, especially to Venice, during the first quarter of the twentieth century, creating etchings modelled on those of the master. While some are of interest as emerging artistic personalities, for the most part their work lacks the freshness, spontaneity and power of invention that Whistler quite rightly believed were all-important. Walter Sickert described Whistler as "a plant with no roots and bearing no fruit",[57] and maintained that "fatherless as he came into the world, so he left it childless."[58]

Nothing could be further from the truth. Looking at printmaking in the aftermath of Whistler's death, it is all too apparent that his influence was all-pervasive, and that for a time his lessons were learnt largely by imitation. He was quite rightly viewed as having made the most important contribution to etching since Rembrandt. In applying his "scientific" analysis of nature to the construction of his compositions, in eliminating all but essential detail, while giving great importance to the space between the lines, and in his concern for fine printing, Whistler swept away centuries of obsession with mechanical hatching, paving the way for the radical experiments of the twentieth century. In the last analysis, even Walter Sickert admired Whistler's unique talents and appreciated "the witty comments of the hand that flew like a swallow over the surface of the copper".[59]

K.L.

1 Val Prinsep, "A Student's Life in Paris in 1859", *The Magazine of Art* 28 (February 1904): 342.

2 Quoted by Linda Nochlin in *Realism and Tradition in Art, 1848-1900* (Englewood Cliffs, New Jersey: Prentice-Hall, 1966), pp. 34-36.

3 Ibid.

4 Quoted by Michael Parkin in *Walter Greaves and The Nocturne* (London: Parkin Gallery, 1974), p. 2.

5 John Ingmells, "Greaves and Whistler," *Apollo* 89 (March 1969): 225.

6 Whistler to the Walter and Harvey Greaves, n.d. (early 1870s), LC PC.

7 Quoted in Elizabeth Robins and Joseph Pennell, *The Life of James McNeill Whistler*, vol. 1 (London: William Heinemann, 2nd ed., 1909), p. 213.

8 Otto Bacher, *With Whistler in Venice* (New York: The Century Co., 1908), p. 39.

9 Pennell, *Life*, vol. 1, p. 290.

10 Walter Sickert, "The New *Life of Whistler*", in *A Free House!* (London: MacMillan and Co. Ltd., 1947), p. 19.

11 Robert Emmons, *The Life and Opinions of Walter Sickert*, (London: Faber and Faber, 1941), p. 206.

12 Mortimer Menpes, *Whistler as I Knew Him* (London: Adam and Charles Black, 1904), p. 24.

13 Ibid., p. 25.

14 Pennell, *Life*, vol. 2, p. 182.

15 Ibid., p. 12.

16 Sickert, "The New *Life of Whistler*," p. 8.

17 Ibid., p. 19.

18 Ibid., pp. 11-12.

19   Quoted by William Rothenstein in *Men and Memories: Recollections of William Rothenstein, 1872-1900*, vol. 1 (London: Faber and Faber, 1931), p. 341.

20   Ibid., p. 169.

21   Ibid., p. 267.

22   Menpes to Whistler, n.d. (1885), GUL BP II 32/21.

23   Sickert to Whistler, n.d. (1885-87), GUL II s/10.

24   Quoted in Pennell, *Life*, vol. 2, p. 71.

25   Ibid.

26   Sickert to Mrs. Whistler, n.d. (December 1888 or January 1889), GUL BP II s/15.

27   Whistler to Menpes, 28 March 1889, GUL BP III G/69.

28   Sickert to Mrs. Whistler, n.d. (1889), GUL BP S/18.

29   Walter Sickert, "L'Affaire Greaves", in *A Free House!*, p. 29.

30   Whistler to Croal Thomson, October 1895, LC PC.

31   Pennell, *Life*, vol. 2, p. 26.

32   Rothenstein, *Men and Memories*, vol. 1, p. 168.

33   Ibid., p. 123.

34   Ibid., p. 268.

35   Joseph Pennell, *The Adventures of an Illustrator* (Boston: Little, Brown and Co., 1925), p. 24.

36   Pennell, *Life*, vol. 2, p. 18.

37   Rothenstein, *Men and Memories*, vol. 1, p. 123.

38   Ibid., p. 267.

39   Ibid., p. 109.

40   Ibid., pp. 109-10.

41   G.H. Boughton, "A Few of the Various Whistlers I have Known", *The Studio* 31 (October 1903): 217.

42   Sickert, " 'Impressonist' Forgeries", in *A Free House!*, p. 40.

43   Whistler to Sickert, n.d. (before 24 November 1896), GUL BP II s/22.

44   Elizabeth Robins and Joseph Pennell, *The Whistler Journal* (Philadelphia: J.B. Lippincott Co., 1921), p. 15.

45   Rothenstein, *Men and Memories*, vol. 1, p. 337.

46   Ibid., p. 338.

47   Walter Shaw Sparrow, *John Lavery and His Work* (London: Kegan Paul, Trench Trübner and Co., [n.d.], p. 158. Quoted in Allen Staley, *From Realism to Symbolism: Whistler and his World* (New York: Columbia University, 1971), p. 22.

48   Pennell, *Life*, vol. 2, p. 220.

49   Pennell, *Whistler Journal*, p. 256.

50   Pennell, *Life*, vol. 2, p. 229.

51   Pennell, *Whistler Journal*, p. 256.

52   Pennell, *Life*, vol. 2, p. 234.

53   Ibid., p. 238-9.

54   Pennell, *Whistler Journal*, p. 228.

55   Pennell, *Whistler Journal*, p. 36.

56   Pennell, *Whistler Journal*, p. 296.

57   Sickert, "From 'Wriggle–and–Chiffon' ", in *A Free House!*, p. 33.

58   Sickert, "Impressionism", in *A Free House!*, p. 26.

59   Sickert, "The New *Life of Whistler*", pp. 12-13.

WHISTLER ETCHINGS

1 *The Unsafe Tenement* from the "French Set" 1858
K. 17 IV/IV
Etching in black ink on *simile japon*
15.9 x 22.7 cm (imp.)
Ex. coll. "E.W." (pencil, *verso*) not in Lugt
Gift of Enid Maclachlan in Memory of
Peter Maclachlan, 1984
Acc. no. 83/5

In mid-August 1858, following the completion of his art studies in Paris, Whistler set out on a journey through Alsace and up the Rhine, accompanied by his bohemian friend, Ernest Delannoy. Hoping to establish his artistic reputation, he planned to complete a series of etchings begun earlier in the year. The series was published in October, 1858, under the title *Twelve Etchings from Nature*, although it has always been known as the "French Set."

The two young artists set out by train, alighting at a number of villages along the route between Nancy and Strasbourg. *The Unsafe Tenement* was originally entitled "*la maison délabré.*"[1] It was made soon after the start of their journey, probably at Liverdun or Maladrie, where Whistler conceived other plates on related themes.

In both subject and style, it reveals the influence of the Barbizon artist Charles Jacque (1813-1894), who was the leading exponent of naturalism in etching, and the most prolific etcher of the day. Looking to the Dutch seventeenth-century tradition, to the etchings of Ruysdael and van Ostade, Jacque created his own rustic vocabulary of dilapidated French farmyards. Whistler would have known the work of Jacque, as well as that of Ruysdael and van Ostade, from the superb collection of etchings formed by his brother-in-law, Francis Seymour Haden.

1 The original title was printed on the uncorrected proof set of the table of contents for *Twelve Etchings from Nature*, 1858, in the Art Institute of Chicago, Brewster Collection of Whistleriana. It is likely, given the latinate ring of the published title, that it was changed at the suggestion of Seymour Haden.

2 *Street at Saverne* from the "French Set" 1858
K. 19 IV/V
Etching in black ink on *chine collé*
20.9 x 15.8 cm (imp.)
Gift of Touche Ross, 1980
Acc. no. 80/27

When Whistler and Ernest Delannoy reached Saverne, Whistler made an elaborate drawing in pencil and coloured wash bearing the annotation, "Place St. Thomas".[1] This formed the basis for the etching, which was made in the course of the journey. In it, Whistler remained remarkably faithful to the drawing, although the etching reproduced the composition in reverse. Areas of wash were translated into areas of dense hatching, creating palpable webs of shadow.

Whistler was by no means the first to see the picturesque beauty in a medieval French streetscape. In the 1820s, fuelled by the Gothic Revival, a group of romantic lithographers, including Eugène Isabey and Richard Parkes Bonington, made superb plates of French medieval streetscapes for Baron Taylor's *Voyages pittoresques et romantiques dans l'ancienne France*. This influential publication continued to appear, volume by volume, from 1820 until 1878.

In the early 1850s the brilliant (if emotionally disturbed) etcher Charles Meryon made haunting etchings of gothic buildings and streetscapes in Paris, which were on the brink of being destroyed by Baron Haussmann's renovations. The sinister feeling created by the projecting house with the high pitched gable recalls the work of Meryon.

While this work undoubtedly looks to the romantic tradition and Meryon for its subject-matter, the choice of a nocturnal setting and the lighting of the composition from within demonstrate Whistler's interest in Rembrandt's etchings, outstanding impressions of which he had ample opportunity to study in the collection of his brother-in-law, Seymour Haden.

The copper plate was printed following Whistler's return

1 *The Unsafe Tenement*, 1858

2 *Street at Saverne*, 1858

to Paris in mid-October by the leading printer of etchings, Auguste Delâtre. Delâtre had developed much of his technical knowledge while printing from Rembrandt's reworked plates, and had experimented in the manner of the Dutch master with the use of plate tone to create *chiaroscuro* effects. This involved leaving residual films of ink on selected areas of the plate, and wiping it clean wherever highlights were wanted. By manipulating the amount of plate tone on the surface of the copper plate, he was able to make the shadow lighter or darker, and the area around the lamp more or less obscure, transforming the time of day from early evening to dark night. By varying the colour of the ink from warm brown to black, and the paper from yellow *japon mince* to blue or grey laid, Delâtre showed Whistler how the tone of the work could be changed from warm to cold, and with it the mood, which became by turns intimate or sinister.

This is an outstanding early proof impression which is very richly inked, and compares very favorably with an impression printed in October 1858, formerly in the collection of Thomas Winans and now at the Metropolitan Museum of Art in New York.

1 See David Curry, *James McNeill Whistler at the Freer Gallery of Art* (New York: Freer Gallery of Art in association with W.W. Norton, 1984), p.167, for a colour reproduction of the drawing.

3 *La Vieille aux loques* from the "French Set" 1858
K. 21 III/III
Etching in black ink on *simile japon*
21.0 x 14.7 cm (imp.)
Gift from the Canadian Imperial Bank of Commerce Fund, 1976
Acc. no. 76/2

In the summer of 1858, Whistler began a series of etchings of Paris working women drawn from the lowest echelon of society. It was interrupted by the "Rhine Journey"

3 *La Vieille aux loques*, 1858

and completed following his return to Paris in October.

He included in this series portraits of tinkers, flower-sellers, dressmakers, and, in this instance, a ragpicker. His sitters tended to be plain, or even ugly, and he went out of his way to make the pretty ones look ordinary. An "objective naturalist," he approached them in a straightforward manner, never idealizing, sentimentalizing, or attempting to endow them with universal significance.[1]

In choosing this subject, Whistler demonstrated his recent affiliation with the Realist movement and its controversial leader, Gustave Courbet. Courbet defended the artist's right to paint lower-class portraits and genre subjects, to clothe his sitters in modern dress, and to use plain or ugly models if he wished. Together with the prominent art critic and poet Charles Baudelaire, he fought the academic tradition entrenched in the Salon: instead of looking toward Raphael and the High Renaissance, they exhorted young artists to look to "modern life" for their subject matter.

In this etching, which was made in October, the calmness and intimacy of the subject, the costume, and the still-life elements, recall paintings of Dutch interiors, as well as those of the eighteenth-century French artist Jean-Baptiste-Siméon Chardin, who was much admired by the Naturalists and Realists. Whistler may also owe a debt to the etchings of peasant women quietly working in shadowed interiors by the Barbizon artist Jean François Millet (1814-1875), which in turn derived from the Dutch tradition.[2]

His interest in the motif of a woman framed by a doorway, thrown into relief by a shadowed interior, was anticipated in etchings made on the Rhine journey. The figure in the doorway was one of the earliest "themes" to enter Whistler's etched work, and one which formed the basis of "variations" in other media. He used this seated profile pose again in *Arrangement in Grey and Black: Portrait of the Artist's Mother* (Y. 187), painted in 1871.

1 Joseph C. Sloane, *French Painting Between the Past and the Present: Artists, Critics and Traditions from 1848-1900* (Princeton: Princeton University Press), p. 74.

2 These had recently been printed by Auguste Delâtre and would have been available at his shop.

4 *The Music Room*   1858
K. 33 I/II
Etching in dark brown ink on old laid paper
14.5 x 21.6 cm (imp.)
Gift from the Canadian Imperial Bank of Commerce Fund, 1976
Acc. no. 76/1

On 6 November 1858, Whistler left for London while the final impressions of his etchings were being pulled by Delâtre in Paris. He went to stay with his brother-in-law, Seymour Haden, a physician who had inherited his father's house and practice in South Kensington (see nos. 45-47). Haden had been asked by Mrs. Whistler to act *in loco parentis* and keep an eye on her son's health, which was somewhat the worse for wear as a result of the Rhine journey.

The set of etchings, generally referred to as the "French Set", was dedicated "*à mon vieil ami, Seymour Haden*" and published from 62 Sloane Street in November. In this way Whistler acknowledged Haden's support and encouragement of his artistic ambitions in the face of parental opposition.

Haden had learnt the basics of the etching technique in the early 1840s at a government art training school in Paris, while studying medicine at the Sorbonne. Following the establishment of his London practice in 1845, he began to build one of the finest collections of etchings in private hands, focusing on Rembrandt and the seventeenth-century Dutch School. This collection had a great influence on Whistler's development.

Haden was eager to try his hand, after seeing Whistler's "French Set", and purchased a press which he installed in a room at the top of the house. During November and December, the brothers-in-law etched side by side, working on related plates and experimenting with artistic printing, exploring the rich *chiaroscuro* effects Delâtre had achieved in the proofs of *Street at Saverne* (no. 2).

Whistler was searching for a middle-class domestic genre subject for his first Salon painting, which he planned to complete following his return to Paris in January 1859. *The Music Room* was probably related to this search; in it he showed Haden and his medical partner James Reeves Traer, reading by lamplight with Whistler's half-sister, Deborah Haden.

Judging by their great variety, he must have enjoyed pulling experimental proofs. He employed different amounts of surface tone on different kinds of paper, creating darker and lighter effects. This impression is very close in ink colour and paper tone to the first impression pulled from the plate on Haden's press, now in the Museum of Fine Arts, Boston. It also compares very favorably with the trial proofs of the first and second states in the British Museum.

5   *Black Lion Wharf* from the "Thames Set" 1859
K. 42 II/III
Etching in black ink on *japon mince*
15.1 x 22.3 cm (imp.)
Gift of Sir Edmund Walker Estate, 1926
Acc. no. 1639

Whistler moved to London in May 1859, with the intention of making it his base of operations. He was an active and enthusiastic member of the "*Société des trois*", which he had formed with Henri Fantin-Latour (1836-1904) and Alphonse Legros (1837-1911) that spring, and which was devoted to creating the art of the future, looking to Courbet and Baudelaire for leadership.

To the Realists, subject was all important, and Whistler set out in search of one that he could make his own. In May he would have seen John Roddam Spencer Stanhope's painting *Thoughts of the Past*, at the Royal Academy, London, with a view of the Thames near Blackfriars in the background.[1] It was not until August that he turned his attention to the Thames after reading Baudelaire's review of the Paris Salon. Baudelaire called for artists to depict "the landscape of great cities," which he felt had been sorely neglected by all but the great etcher Charles Meryon.[2]

It was but one short step to do for London what Meryon had done for Paris, and to create realist views along the Thames as Meryon had done along the Seine. After making a modest start around Westminster, Whistler began to explore the docks of Wapping and Rotherhithe. The neighbourhood was rough and unsavoury, and the river little more than a cesspool. Nonetheless, from early August to early October, the young Realist went to live there and become thoroughly immersed in the life of the area.

While Whistler's Thames etchings of 1859 appear superficially as landscapes with warehouses in the background, he placed the men who worked on the river front and centre, where they could not be viewed as incidental, and made them disproportionately large like Courbet's working men. The subject was modern, working-class, combined the elements of seascape and cityscape, and was, above all, novel. When Whistler began work on his painting, *Wapping* (Y. 35), the following year, he went to great pains to make sure that his friends did not tell Courbet, for fear that the latter might steal the subject.

Black Lion Wharf was made looking toward the North Bank, possibly from the Horselydown New Stairs. While most of the area has since been demolished, the great Hoare and Company warehouse still stands, its painted sign dimly visible, just to the east of the St. Katharine's Dock. Whistler reversed this plate, to make the subject appear the same way round as it does in nature, and must have gone to great pains over it.

His approach to the subject demonstrates an important new phase in his theoretical development. During the summer of 1859 he had moved away from the more conventional representation of picture space which he had used in the "French Set." Instead of receding in depth, *Black Lion Wharf* is flattened, and the illusion of recession is achieved through the placement of a large *repoussoir* figure in the foreground plane, diagonal directional lines in the middle ground, and a high horizon line in the background. The figure is placed in the immediate foreground where it becomes the focus of the composition, and arrests the eye before allowing it to stray into the landscape background. *Black Lion Wharf* is one of the most important works in Whistler's entire *oeuvre*; in it, his new system of constructing picture space was fully realised.

Whistler's Thames etchings of 1859 took on the appearance and tonality of contemporary landscape photographs. The early lens was unable to suggest the depth of field found in nature, and the background seemed to hang like a theatrical drop. Whistler selected one area of the composition as a focal point, and left those areas which fell into the field of peripheral vision unworked or barely indicated. This was the beginning of the process of elimination, which continued to evolve with his changing aesthetic, until his works were popularly considered "jokes" on account of their lack of "finish".

4 *The Music Room*

5 *Black Lion Wharf*, 1859

Whistler thought very highly of this etching, and placed it on the wall of his studio; it appears in the background of *Arrangement in Grey and Black: Portrait of the Artist's Mother* (Y. 101), of 1871.

This is an outstanding impression on thin golden Japanese paper. It was acquired by Sir Edmund Walker, founder of the Art Gallery of Ontario, from the New York dealer Frederick Keppel in 1897.

1 This connection was first suggested by Robin Spencer in "Whistler's Subject Matter: 'Wapping' 1860-64," *Gazette des Beaux Arts* VI (October 1962): 135.

2 Charles Baudelaire, "The Salon of 1859", in *Art in Paris, 1845-1862: Salons and Other Exhibitions, Reviewed by Charles Baudelaire*. Trans. and ed. by Jonathan Mayne (London: Phaidon Press, 1965), p. 200.

6   *Longshoremen* 1859
K. 45, only state
Etching in black ink on old laid paper
15.2 x 22.7 cm (imp.)
Gift of the Edmund Morris Estate, 1913
Acc. no. 476

As members of the "*Société des trois*," Alphonse Legros and Whistler shared little but their interest in etching, and probably sent impressions of their latest work back and forth with Fantin when he visited Whistler in London in July.

Legros used an undisciplined scratchy drypoint line and drew with deliberate awkwardness. The *naïveté* of his Salon painting, *The Angelus*, had been praised by Baudelaire in his review in July 1859; this greatly impressed Whistler and Fantin, whose submissions had both been rejected. Legros was in turn inspired by Courbet, who had built such elements into his paintings, and was roundly criticized for them. *Naïveté* was to become a dominant characteristic of Realist etching.

Whistler made *Longshoremen*, which employed similar naïve elements, while working at Wapping in the autumn. The character of the line reflects the harsh environment and life of the working men who loaded and unloaded ships in the London docks.

This impression was included in the *Loan Exhibition…of Works in Black and White and in Sanguine* held at the Art Museum of Toronto (now Art Gallery of Ontario) in April-May 1912.

6 *Longshoremen*, 1859

7   *Soupe à Trois Sous* 1859
K. 49, only state
Drypoint in black ink on double *chine collé*
with plate tone
15.2 x 22.7 cm (imp.)
Purchase, 1983
Acc. no. 83/21

Whistler left for Paris on 6 October 1859 and remained there until shortly before Christmas. During this time he experimented with drypoint for the first time.

Shortly after arriving in Paris, he made *Soupe à trois sous* in an all-night café. The low-life subject, naïve drawing, and construction of the picture space, recall the Thames etching *Longshoremen* (no. 6). The figure on the left, who is the focus of attention, was a former soldier named Martin who had lost the cross of the Legion of Honour because of misconduct. A sinister element is injected into the sordid surroundings by the black bottles at the elbows of the men who sleep seated or sprawling across the tables.

This is a most unusual impression, printed with plate tone on grey-mauve double *chine collé*. Peter Zegers, who has examined this impression, pointed out that "the support consists of two layers of india-proof paper (chine) of different hues and dimensions, laminated together and superimposed onto a third…rigid support".[1]

1 Peter Zegers to the author, 7 May 1984, Accession File, Art Gallery of Ontario.

7 *Soupe à Trois Sous*, 1859

8   *Bibi Lalouette* 1859
K. 51 II/II
Etching and drypoint in black ink on silk satin
22.8 x 15.3 cm (imp.)
Gift of the Dorothy Isabella Webb Trust
in memory of Sir Edmund Walker,
first President of the Art Gallery of Ontario
(1900-1924), 1982
Acc. no. 83/4

Most of the drypoints Whistler made in Paris in the autumn of 1859 were portraits of children, the artist or his friends. One of the first was the child of a restaurant owner who had extended Whistler a line of credit during his student days.

8 *Bibi Lalouette*, 1859

The delicacy of handling in *Bibi Lalouette* demonstrates Whistler's mastery of linear expression of all kinds. His line is as refined in this plate as it is crude in the two that precede it in this catalogue. It is very likely that he chose to match the character of his line to the nature of his subject.

This impression was probably printed at Seymour Haden's home in London over Christmas. It is unique in that it is the only known impression of a work by Whistler printed on silk. When it is looked at in raking light, a disembodied network of black lines appears to float on a silvery ground, enhancing the elegance and refinement of the piece. Whistler's use of silk was undoubtedly inspired by Rembrandt's occasional use of it for trial proofs.

9   *Drouet* 1859
K. 55 II/II
Drypoint in black ink on modern laid paper
22.6 x 15.0 cm (imp.)
Ex. coll. "A.K." (pencil, *verso*) not in Lugt
Gift of Mr. and Mrs. Ralph Presgrave, 1976
Acc. no. 76/238

The finest portrait Whistler made in Paris in the autumn of 1859 was that of his friend, the sculptor Charles Drouet, who apparently sat for him for several hours. Whistler omit-

ted much of the peripheral detail, focusing on the face while barely indicating costume and setting. This plate not only demonstrates his continuing interest in focus, it also reveals his interest in seventeenth-century Dutch portrait etching, particularly the work of Van Dyck and Rembrandt.

Whistler would have been familiar with Van Dyck's series of etchings of friends and fellow artists, published under the title *Iconographia*, as Seymour Haden had an outstanding group of early states in his collection. Haden, like others before and since, lamented the fact that after drawing the heads in detail and indicating the torso with a few lines, van Dyck turned the plates over to professional engravers who "finished" them. Whistler's *Drouet* recalls van Dyck's unfinished portraits in the treatment of the head and torso, as well as in the baroque vigour and dash that characterize the heavy slashing strokes and hairline hatching.

Since drypoint lines wear down quickly, few impressions could be pulled from this plate. Whistler loved it and hoarded his impressions. Most, including this one, were made after the plate had been cancelled in 1879, and the cancellation mark successfully removed.

10   *The Forge* from the "Thames Set" 1861
K. 68 IV/IV
Drypoint on laid paper
18.8 x 31 cm (imp.)
Gift of Mr. and Mrs. Ralph Presgrave, 1976
Acc. no. 76/239

Whistler became seriously ill with rheumatic fever in June 1861. Following his recovery he went to Brittany, remaining there from the beginning of September to the end of the first week in November.

During this period he made a drypoint, *The Forge*, at Perros-Guirec, which recalls François Bonvin's (1817-1887) Brittany painting *Les Forgerons: Souvenir du Treport*, exhibited at the Salon of 1857. Whistler treated the subject, which was a favorite with the Romantics and Realists, in a new way. Gone were the straining, Vulcan-like muscles found in the work of his predecessors; Whistler's smith stands like an alchemist before the forge observing the glowing metal, while apprentices stand by watching the transfor-

9 *Drouet*, 1859

10 *The Forge* from the "Thames Set", 1861

mation take place. In *The Forge*, nature is rendered alternately substantial and insubstantial as the glowing metal goes through its metamorphosis.

In this plate, he returned to the theme of lighting the picture space from within, which he had explored in *The Music Room* three years earlier (no. 4). He was no longer concerned with social messages *per se*; rather, he was much more interested in *tenebroso* lighting effects, the drama of shifting illumination, and the way in which forms were rendered ambiguous by firelight.

He was to return to this subject in his etchings and lithographs again and again (nos. 38 and 39). Whistler was very pleased with this drypoint and printed all the early impressions himself, often on thin, silky *japon mince*.

11 '*The Adam and Eve'*, *Old Chelsea* 1879
K. 175 II/II
Etching in black ink on *japon mince*
17.3 x 30.2 cm (imp.)
Gift of Inco Limited, 1984
Acc. no. 83/6

Whistler made this plate of the Chelsea waterfront, and a number of large etchings of bridges over the Thames near Chelsea, when he was faced with impending bankruptcy in the spring of 1879.

The publication of his Thames etching *Billingsgate* (K. 47, 1859), in the *Portfolio* magazine in January 1878, probably gave him the idea of producing large, attractive etchings for the marketplace, catering to the tastes of those who had admired his "Thames Set." He hoped that he could make enough money from their sale to pay his mounting pile of debts and to allow him to go to Venice to make a series of etchings.

Early in 1879 the first of the new etchings, *"The Adam and Eve," Old Chelsea*, was published by Messrs. Hogarth and Son. The old waterfront tavern had been demolished to make way for the Chelsea embankment, and it seems very likely that Whistler worked from a photograph by the Chelsea photographer James Hedderly as well as from memory.[1] In doing so he was undoubtedly catering to the nostalgia market.

In *"The Adam and Eve," Old Chelsea*, Whistler's con-

cern was not so much to describe the physical character of the structure as to capture the feeling of light and atmosphere in a composition based on oriental principles of balance and placement. In his early Thames plates, as he pointed out to his biographers, Joseph and Elizabeth Pennell, he drew every plank, every brick, and every roofing tile, with a firm, unbroken contour. In this plate, he suggested light by means of shadow, and the whole by means of a part. In it the eye is no longer drawn to a specific area of the composition; instead, it is attracted to different areas wherever details congregate.

He was later to see this as the key transitional work in his evolution from the realist style of the Thames etchings of 1859 to the "impressionist" style of the Venice etchings of 1879-80.[2]

1   I am indebted to Robin Spencer for pointing out to me that the Adam and Eve had been demolished by the time this plate was made. Robin Spencer and Nigel Thorp advised me of the possible link with the Hedderley photographs.

2   Elizabeth Robins and Joseph Pennell, *The Life of James McNeill Whistler*, vol. 1 (London: William Heinemann, 1909), p. 281.

12   *Hurlingham*
K. 181 III/III
Etching on laid paper
13.2 x 20.2 cm (imp.)
Gift of Mr. and Mrs. James Dickinson, 1985
Acc. no. 85/279

Like *"The Adam and Eve": Old Chelsea* (no. 11), this plate was made at Fulham during the spring of 1879 when Whistler was trying desperately to stave off bankruptcy. It fits into a group of picturesque Thames views, made in the vicinity of Chelsea and Fulham, which catered to the nostalgia market and to the tastes of those who preferred his Thames etchings of 1879 to the slight productions of the mid-1870s.

Hurlingham was published by The Printsellers' Association. Despite the revenue from the sale of this and the other plates, Whistler was declared bankrupt in May 1879.

11 *'The Adam and Eve', Old Chelsea, 1879*

12 *Hurlingham*

13 *Nocturne* from "The First Venice Set" 1879-80
K. 184 IV/V
Etching and drypoint printed in warm brown ink
with plate tone on old laid paper
24 x 29.5 cm (imp.)
Trimmed to the plate marked and signed on the tab
with a butterfly
Gift of Touche Ross, 1978
Acc. no. 77/190

The publication of the Thames etchings was not adequate to meet Whistler's growing pile of debts. In May 1879 he was declared bankrupt, and his house and possessions were seized by bailiffs. Fortunately, he was commissioned by the Fine Art Society to go to Venice in September to make a series of twelve etched views.

One of the most important "themes" Whistler explored in Venice was that of the city "floating" on the lagoon. Ruskin had described the city in words that were etched into the minds of Whistler's generation as "a ghost upon the sands of the sea, so weak – so quiet – so bereft of all but her loveliness, that we might well doubt as we watched her faint reflections in the mirage of the lagoon, which was the City, and which the Shadow."[1]

The greatest "variation" was *Nocturne*, made partly from nature and partly from memory. Using the same etched matrix, which contained the framework of the composition, Whistler printed each impression using different amounts of plate tone; by wiping the ink with muslin and his palm, he created a variety of nocturnal effects of greater or lesser intensity. He was also able, by varying the tone of the ink from black to brown, to change the temperature, mood and time of day.

Most impressions, such as this one, capture the effects of twilight, and have a "clearing" on the horizon against which San Giorgio and the large ship are silhouetted as the last rays of the sun slowly fade. In a handful of darker impressions, the forms blend and flow into one another before they are finally swallowed up by darkness. In the blackest impession, only the last hint of light is visible along the horizon as night descends.

Whistler's interest in changing the time of day and capturing the magic of the floating city inevitably recalls the work of Joseph Mallord William Turner (1775-1851). His early love of Turner appears to have resurfaced in the 1870s, along with his interest in capturing the poetry of nature and atmospheric effect. The fluid way in which Whistler applied plate tone to give his etched nocturnes translucency recalls Turner's magnificent watercolour "notes" of Venice. Nowhere is this more apparent than in this evening view of the Isola di S. Giorgio Maggiore and the Basilica della Salute seen from the Riva degli Schiavoni.

Whistler's decision to experiment with plate tone, after twenty years of avoidance, enabled him to create luminous nocturnal effects. His successful lithotint *Nocturne: The River at Battersea* of 1878 (no. 23) probably had something to do with this decision, although there are several other theories.[2]

1 John Ruskin, *The Stones of Venice: Introductory Chapters and Local Indices for the Use of Travellers while Staying in Venice and Verona* (New York: D.D. Merrill Co. 1879), p. 144.

2 See Katharine Lochnan, *The Etchings of James McNeill Whistler* (New Haven and London: Yale University Press, 1984), pp. 196-211.

14 *The Riva No. 1* from "The First Venice Set" 1879
K. 192 III/III
Etching in brown/black ink on old laid paper
20.0 x 29.5 cm (sheet)
Trimmed to the plate line and signed on the tab
with a butterfly
Presented by Friends of S.V. Blake, Esq., 1925,
in memory of him
Acc. no. 772

At the beginning of the summer of 1880, Whistler met a group of students who had recently spent the winter in Florence studying under Frank Duveneck (1848-1919), an American painter of German descent. It was not long before Duveneck and his "boys" ran into Whistler, who was delighted to find himself surrounded by young admirers.

Chief among them was Otto Bacher (1856-1909), an etcher who had brought with him a portable press from Munich. Bacher persuaded Whistler and his common-law wife Maud Franklin to move to the room next to his in the Casa Jancovitz at the end of the Riva degli Schiavoni near the Via Garibaldi. The move may have been occasioned partly by financial necessity, but brought with it the advantages of an excellent view of the Doge's Palace, San Giorgio and the Salute, as well as the congenial company of Bacher and his friends and easy access to Bacher's etching press.

The Riva, No. 1 was probably etched from the windows in the Casa Jancovitz looking along the Riva degli Schiavoni toward San Marco, the domes of which are visible near the right-hand margin of the plate. The composition was inspired by an etching by Frank Duveneck, *The Riva, Look-*

13 *Nocturne*, 1879-80
See colour plate on page 8

14 *The Riva No. 1*, 1879

ing Towards the Grand Ducal Palace, although the latter was made closer to San Marco. Upon seeing Duveneck's etching, Whistler said "Whistler must do the Riva also."[1]

The Royal Academy had consistently refused to admit painter-etchers, unlike reproductive engravers, to full membership. While Whistler was in Venice, his estranged brother-in-law, Seymour Haden, founded the Society of Painter-Etchers as an alternative. Whistler bitterly resented the position that Haden had assumed as the chief spokesman for etching in England, and campaigned vigorously to keep his friends, among them Otto Bacher, from submitting work to the first exhibition.

Haden, whose vision may have begun to fail, apparently mistook the etchings of Venice submitted by Frank Duveneck for those of Whistler. Not having heard of Duveneck, and suspecting that Whistler had adopted a *nom de plume* in order to submit work to the Painter Etchers, Haden paid a visit to the Fine Art Society and demanded to see Whistler's new Venice etchings. Whistler was incensed when he heard about this, and attacked Haden in *The Piker Papers*, asking whether it was "officially as the Painter-Etchers' President that you pry about the town?"[2]

1 Otto Bacher, *With Whistler in Venice* (New York: The Century Co., 1908), p. 144.

2 Whistler "La Suite", in *The Gentle Art of Making Enemies* (London: William Heinemann, 1890), p. 59.

15 *Nocturne: Palaces* from "The Second Venice Set"
1879-80
K. 202 VII/IX
Etching and drypoint printed with plate tone on old laid paper
29.6 x 20.1 cm
Trimmed to the plate line and signed on the tab with a butterfly
Gift of Esther and Arthur Gelber, 1982
Acc. no. 82/45

In Venice, Whistler came into his own. He finally created the synthesis for which he had been searching, combining his love of picturesque form and spatial geometry learned from the Dutch, with the two-dimensional decorative patterns learnt from Japanese prints. The placement of the fragments became increasingly more refined, and the subtle sense of balance more exact. In the Venice etchings, his poetic impressions were suspended like a veil before the viewer, and nature was transformed into delicate compositional arrangements of pattern and void which were flattened until they hung midway between two and three dimensions.

For the most part, Whistler avoided the views immortalized by his illustrious forebears, Canaletto, Guardi and Turner, who were very much on his mind. He sought out picturesque nooks and crannies on the smaller canals to which the old masters had not penetrated. These provided endless opportunities for frontal close-ups, with water in the foreground and ornamental doorways in the middle distance, hinting at mysterious inner depths.

In *Nocturne: Palaces*, arguably Whistler's most beautiful etching, the line once again provided only the most elementary grid for the effects to be achieved by artistic printing. The time of day and temperature varied with the inking: black ink gave the plate a cool feeling, while brown ink gave it a warm one. By leaving progressively more brown ink on the plate, Whistler could suggest a summer evening, a soft warm night, or a hot dark night.

15 *Nocturne: Palaces*, 1879-80
See colour plate on page 2

16 *Upright Venice,* 1879-80

He used a lamp to light the composition from within, a device borrowed from Rembrandt, which he had used for the first time in *Street at Saverne* in 1858 (no. 2). In some impressions, by varying the inking, the lamp is made to appear very bright, while in others it can scarcely be seen. The brighter the rays that emanate from it, the less visible the bridge becomes, being thrust into shadow. The intensity of the reflections cast by the door and boat on the canal also vary from one impression to another, the most dramatic having the strongest reflections. The evening mist descends from above in vertical striations, which at times look almost like rain.

In this outstanding impression Whistler captured the mood of a warm summer evening.

16 *Upright Venice* from "The Second Venice Set"
1879-80
K. 205 III/IV
Etching in warm black ink on old laid paper
25.3 x 17.7 cm
Trimmed to the plate line and signed on the tab with a butterfly
Gift of Sir Edmund Walker Estate, 1926
Acc. no. 1638

In Venice, Whistler continued to draw shadows rather than contours, using infinite numbers of hairlike lines running roughly parallel to each other, sandwiching the shimmering light between them. In this way he achieved in etching what he later called "painting with exquisite line".

He continued to explore themes and variations that had preoccupied him for years, demonstrating the consistency of his formal concerns. While his subjects are attractive and capture the feeling of the city, he was not interested in subject as an end in itself, and did not reverse his plates. His interest lay in the more purely abstract elements of the composition; subject-matter played an increasingly incidental role.

It is not known exactly when Whistler first encountered Japanese woodcuts. In 1862 he began to purchase them in Paris, and by 1864 he had begun to incorporate overtly Japanese motifs into his paintings. His picture space became more and more two-dimensional as he transformed it in the light of this new influence. From this time to the end of his life, oriental influence took pride of place in his evolving aesthetic.

In *Upright Venice*, which was probably made from the window of the Casa Jancovitz at the end of the Riva degli Schiavoni, Whistler flattened the picture space, and used the diagonal wedge of the Riva in the foreground to lead the eye across the lagoon to the horizon line, where the domes of Santa Maria Maggiore are clearly visible at the mouth of the Grand Canal. The compositional format had become a "theme" on which Whistler worked a Venetian "variation." This set of compositional devices, frequently found in Hiroshige, was first used by Whistler in 1866 in the painting *The Morning after the Revolution, Valparaiso* (Y. 75).

17 *Swan and Iris* 1883
K. 241 I/III
Etching in warm black ink on old laid paper
15.8 x 9.4 cm (sheet)
Signed with the butterfly
Gift of Sir Edmund Walker Estate, 1926
Acc. no. 1517

Swan and Iris is typical of the small views of London that Whistler etched after his return from Venice. It was made after a painting by the late Cecil Lawson (1849-1882), and was published in *Cecil Lawson, a Memoir*, written by Edmund Gosse, in 1883. It is unique in Whistler's *oeuvre*, being the only reproductive print he made after a work by another artist. As such, it was a great tribute to Lawson.

Whistler, along with many of his contemporaries, greatly regretted the premature death of the young and talented artist. J. Comyns Carr wrote, "Whistler exalted with Cecil Lawson at his success at the Grosvenor Gallery after not being very well received at the Academy. The 'Pastoral' and the 'Minister's Garden' set him, at a bound, in the front rank of the painters of his time."[1]

1 J. Comyns Carr, *Some Eminent Victorians* (London: Duckworth, 1908), p. 137.

17 *Swan and Iris*, 1883

18 *Fragment of Piccadilly* 1884-86
K. 256, only state
Etching in warm black ink with plate tone on old laid paper
11.0 x 7.0 cm (sheet)
Trimmed to the plate mark and signed on the tab
with a butterfly
Gift of Sir Edmund Walker Estate, 1926
Acc. no. 1632

Following Whistler's return from Venice, most of his energy was devoted to the printing of the Venice etchings. At the same time, he managed to begin a series of small plates of London streetscapes. By comparison with the Venice etchings, Whistler's London plates seem excessively modest both in scale and in scope. For Whistler, etching and sketching had become interchangeable: he carried around grounded copper plates and used them for jotting down visual impressions as if they were sheets in a sketchbook. The maximum size of the plates was in large measure determined by the dimensions of his coat pocket.

The minimal shorthand description of architecture and human form found in *Fragment of Piccadilly* is characteristic of the London plates. In 1886 Whistler codified his ideas about etching into eleven "Propositions" which were published with the "Second Venice Set." In them he addressed a number of key questions about the scale of the etching needle to the copper plate, and of the paper margin to the etched composition. In the London plates, he observed his margins to the letter.

It is in these plates that Whistler's "impressionist" style was distilled and codified. These quintessential statements inspired endless imitations by the "followers," including Walter Sickert (no. 61) and Theodore Roussel (no. 59), and by those who mistakenly believed them to be easy to replicate.

18 *Fragment of Piccadilly*, 1884-86

19 *Seats, Gray's Inn* 1886-88
K. 299, only state
Etching in warm black ink on old laid paper
8.3 x 17.8 cm (sheet)
Trimmed to the plate mark and signed on the tab
with a butterfly
Gift of Sir Edmund Walker Estate, 1926
Acc. no. 1633

With the intention of issuing a "Gray's Inn Set",[1] Whistler made several plates in the quiet legal precinct of Bloomsbury, which still looks very much the same today, with its lawns, gravel paths, benches and gas lamps. The plates show mothers and children resting or playing in the gardens. The subject-matter, together with the light and airy treatment, suggest that Whistler was well aware of the etchings of the French Impressionists. Monet and Pissarro were among his friends and admirers at this time.

This impression demonstrates the physical appearance Whistler sought in his late plates. In the 1880s, according to Mortimer Menpes, "Whistler wiped his plates cleanly; the lines were less full, less charged with ink: the ideal proofs of the period were suggestive of ivory."[2]

1 Ledger Book, GUL BP.

2 Mortimer Menpes, *Whistler as I Knew Him* (London: Adam and Charles Black, 1904), p. 96.

20 *Dry Dock, Southampton*
from "The Naval Review Series" 1887
K. 322, only state
Etching in black ink on old laid paper
6.4 x 17.4 cm (imp.)
Trimmed to the plate mark and signed on the tab
with a butterfly
Gift of Sir Edmund Walker Estate, 1926
Acc. no. 1516

As President of the Society of British Artists, Whistler received a number of official invitations in 1887 on the occasion of Queen Victoria's Jubilee. *The Naval Review* or *Jubilee Series* was etched during the Naval Review off Spithead on July 27. The plates were made for the most part on a moving boat and were completed the next day. In this series of twelve etchings the teachings embedded in the "Propositions" of 1886 were followed to the letter.

Whistler referred to these sprightly little plates as "notes of the needle",[1] and printed them in a very small edition which was sent to the dealer, Dowdeswells, in August and September. They were among the last etchings made by Whistler in England.

1 Whistler to the Rt. Hon. Smith, First Lord of the Treasury, 1 December 1887, Library of Congress, Pennell Collection.

19 *Seats, Gray's Inn*, 1886-88

20 *Dry Dock, Southampton*, 1887

21 *Long House – Dyers – Amsterdam*, 1889
K. 406 III/III
Etching and drypoint printed in brown ink on
Japanese paper
15.4 x 27.0 cm (sheet)
Gift of Mr. Arthur Gelber, in memory of
Mrs. Esther Gelber, 1985
Acc. no. 85/112

For many years Whistler had expressed a desire to go to Amsterdam "to portray with their fascinating reflections some of the picturesque old houses on the canals" of Rembrandt's city.[1] He finally went in August 1889, intending to make a series of copper plates. He worked from a boat in back canals, where he had some unpleasant encounters when locals, resenting his presence, emptied the contents of buckets out of windows onto his head.

In Amsterdam, as in London and Venice, Whistler adopted a frontal close-up approach to façades, keeping the canal in the foreground. The buildings tend to hang like a curtain in the middle distance. It was in these etchings Whistler that came closest to flattening his picture space. *Long House – Dyers – Amsterdam* is one of the most beautiful of the Amsterdam etchings, and demonstrates to perfection Whistler's virtuoso technique for describing reflections.

In these plates, Whistler worked over the entire surface of the grounded copper plate with a network of minute hair-like lines, leaving no space uncovered. Hardly any ground remained, and the lines ran together when the plates were bitten in acid. They wore very quickly under the pressure of the press, and only a handful of impressions were pulled before the plates began to go gray and bald.

These etchings were at the same time Whistler's most splendid and most overblown productions; in them he pushed the etching technique beyond the physical limits of the medium. It was no doubt with the Amsterdam etchings in mind that Walter Sickert referred to Whistler's "feast of facile and dainty sketching on copper."[2]

The result, however, was to produce extraordinary *chiaroscuro* effects in which light and dark were carefully modulated to give the overall surface a new vitality and visual richness. These etchings are themselves mirrored surfaces, veneers and façades. In them, Whistler magically transformed the disjointed structures into palaces by capturing their pattern and colour and mirrored reflections. Like his new friend, the poet Stéphane Mallarmé, he sought to capture the essence of what was otherwise impermanent in nature. He returned to the use of Rembrandtesque *chiaroscuro*, which he had mastered in the "French Set," and combined it with design elements learnt from the study of Japanese prints. Rejecting plate tone, he learnt to "paint with exquisite line," creating multifaceted images which shimmer with light and "colour."

When George Bernard Shaw saw the Amsterdam plates on exhibit in 1890, he called them " 'the most exquisite renderings by the most independent man of the century' " and added, " 'Had Mr. Whistler never put brush to canvas, he has done enough in these plates to be able to say that he will not altogether die.' "[3]

1 Howard Mansfield, *Whistler in Belgium and Holland* (New York: Knoedler and Co., n.d.).

2 Walter Sickert, "Round and About Whistler", in *A Free House!* (London: MacMillan and Co. Ltd., 1947), p. 11.

3 Pennell, *Life*, vol. 2, p. 86.

21 *Long House – Dyers – Amsterdam*, 1889

WHISTLER LITHOGRAPHS

22 *Limehouse*, 1878
W. 4, L. 8 II/II
Lithotint on *chine collé*
17.2 x 26.4 cm (image)
Signed in pencil in lower right margin "Whistler"
Gift of Norcen Energy Resources Limited, 1979
Acc. no. 79/21

In the early 1870s, Whistler was preoccupied with describing atmospheric effect in etching using line, but found it very difficult. He did not resort to plate tone, with which he had achieved superb nocturnal effects in his etchings of 1858 (no. 2 and 4), probably because it had come to be considered the refuge of the amateur etcher trying to cover poor linework. It was therefore fortunate that in 1878 he met the lithographic printer Thomas R. Way, the only printer left in England who was concerned to revive artistic lithography. Hoping to provide Whistler with a graphic medium in which to express the poetic effects he had achieved in painting the Thames nocturnes in the early 1870s, Way introduced the artist to the unusual process of lithotint, which allowed him to paint on the stone using diluted lithographic inks. It proved an ideal medium for describing atmospheric effect.

Tom Way, the son of T.R. Way, recalled how he was sent to see Whistler at 96 Lindsay Row with a message about "the arrangements for an excursion down the river with my father for the next drawing – 'Limehouse.' "[1] In order to assist Whistler in working from nature, T.R. Way supplied "barges, barrows and porters" to convey the heavy lithographic stone to Limehouse, and sat next to him on a barge while he worked.[2]

In this lithotint, Whistler worked close to the place where his first Thames etchings were made (no. 5). He was no longer interested in making a portrait of the tumbledown bankside buildings; instead, he sought to capture the essence of the place and the appearance of the ensemble on an overcast day when the forms ran together. What they lost in distinctness they gained in mood. He worked from light to dark and dark to light, scratching highlights out of the dark passages. The richness of the blacks recalls the work

of the French romantic lithographers of the 1830s, and of the English mezzotints that inspired them.

After he had placed the drawing on the stone, it was hauled back to Way's shop at 21 Wellington St. in the Strand, where Whistler added the figures, which were drawn from people walking in the street outside the window. When first proved, the image came out heavy and flat, and Whistler repeatedly retouched it until he was satisfied.[3] The drawing required much retracing on the stone.[4]

Plans for the first publication of Whistler's lithographs were conceived by Way at this time. Signed and mounted proofs of Limehouse were offered for sale for one guinea each. There was, however, a very poor response to the circular, and fewer than five orders were received.[5] As a result, only half a dozen impressions were pulled in 1878-79. An edition of 30 was made by Way in 1887 for publication in *Art Notes*; this impression comes from the second edition.

1 T.R. Way, *Memories of James McNeill Whistler* (London: John Lane, 1912), p. 10.

2 Joseph Pennell, "Artistic Lithography," *Journal of the Royal Society of Arts*, 62 (20 July 1914): 732.

3 Way, *Memories*, p. 12.

4 Way, "Mr. Whistler as a Lithographer," *The Studio* 30 (1903-1904): 14.

5 Way, *Memories*, p. 16.

---

23 *Nocturne: The River at Battersea*, 1878
W. 5, L. 11 I/II
Lithotint on blue-grey *chine collé*
17.2 x 25.8 cm (image)
Signed in pencil in lower right margin "Whistler"
Ex. coll. Henry H. Benedict (Lugt 2936)
Gift of Mr. Arthur Gelber
in memory of Mrs. Esther Gelber, 1984
Acc. no. 84/67

During the 1860s, Whistler abandoned Realism for Aestheticism. While he continued to employ many of the same subjects that he had addressed earlier in painting and etching, he treated them quite differently. He was no longer interested in nature viewed in the clear light of day with all its imperfections; he was interested instead in the way in which it is transformed by mist and fog, twilight and darkness, and the abstract beauty that emerges when forms blend together. The industrial reaches of the Thames were soon transformed by veils of mist and darkness.

It was in the early 1870s that Whistler created the Thames nocturnes in painting for which he is justly famous. In order to prepare himself to paint nocturnal effects, he would row on the river at night, and commit the details to memory using the method taught by Lecoq de Boisbaudran (1802-1897). The synthesis that emerged was very much his own, and while his work was still based on nature, it was nature distilled by the imagination and poetic sensibility. Whistler described his changed approach to nature in a

22 *Limehouse*, 1878

passage in his "Ten O'Clock" lecture of 1885, in which he wrote:

And when the evening mist clothes the riverside with poetry, as with a veil, and the poor buildings lose themselves in the dim sky, and the tall chimneys become campanili, and the warehouses are palaces in the night, and the whole city hangs in the heavens, and fairy-land is before us – then the wayfarer hastens home; the working man and the cultured one, the wise one and the one of pleasure, cease to understand, as they have ceased to see, and Nature, who, for once, has sung in tune, sings her exquisite song to the artist alone, her son and her master – her son in that he loves her, her master in that he knows her.[1]

The lithotint process was perfectly suited to capturing the veiled effects Whistler achieved in his painted nocturnes. *Nocturne: The River at Battersea* shows the view of the river from Whistler's window on Lindsay Row, now Cheyne Walk. The industrial shoreline, which included saw mills, a timber yard, turpentine works, chemical works, flour mills, and the church of St. Mary, was magically tranformed at night.[2] The print was made from memory "at one effort", using thin washes of invisible lithographic ink on a stone prepared with an area of half tint by Way. It needed only slight retouching.[3] Proved on delicate Japanese paper mounted on plate paper, *Nocturne* was then printed on a cool grey paper "as giving more closely the tone intended."[4] Like *Limehouse* (no. 22), it was conceived as part of a series to be issued monthly, and finally appeared in *Art Notes* in 1887. One hundred proofs were printed; this is one of the finest pulled.

There was so little commercial interest at the time that Whistler, who was on the verge of bankruptcy, made no more lithotints, and turned instead to large etchings of the river (see no. 11). The artistic success of this work must have contributed to his decision to use plate tone in his Venice etchings of 1879-80. Both the composition and technique anticipate the etching *Nocturne* (no. 13). Way forever afterwards tried to encourage Whistler to return to lithotint. Although two others were made, the first two are arguably the finest.

1 "Mr. Whistler's 'Ten O'Clock' ", in *The Gentle Art of Making Enemies* (London: William Heinemann, 1890), p. 144.

2 See *Stanford's New Map of London and its Suburbs*, 1862.

3 Way, *Memories*, p. 16.

4 Way, *Memories*, p. 17.

23 *Nocturne: The River at Battersea*, 1878
See colour plate (detail) on the cover

24 *Gants de suède* from *The Studio* 1890
W. 26, L. 40
Transfer lithograph on wove paper
29.6 x 21.1 cm (sheet)
Gallery Purchase, 1923
Acc. no. 742

Whistler gave up lithography from 1879 to 1887, preferring to concentrate on etching instead. When he did return to it, he was freed from the necessity of drawing directly on stone by Tom Way, who introduced him to the use of transfer paper. This involved drawing with special chalks on prepared paper, which came in tablets as portable as the small etching plates he put in his pocket. When Whistler moved to Paris in 1892, it was relatively easy for him to roll up his drawings on transfer paper in large periodicals and send them to Way in London. After transferring them to the stone by a secret method, Way would dispatch proofs for Whistler's comments by return post.

Whistler's increasing devotion to the lithographic technique in the period 1887-96 had roots in his personal life. In 1888 he married Beatrice Godwin (*née* Birnie Philip), the widow of E.W. Godwin, the architect of Whistler's White House. Beatrice, who was herself an artist, actively encouraged her husband to explore lithography, being convinced that he would do great things in it.

Gants de suède is a portrait of Beatrice's sister Ethel Philip, who was nicknamed "Bunnie" by Whistler. It may have been executed as a *première pensée* for the painting *Harmony in Brown: The Felt Hat* (Y. 395), which Théodore Duret saw in progress in London in 1891. The costume and pose in both lithograph and painting are very similar.[1]

Like his friend Fantin-Latour, who said "my drawings are my lithographs," Whistler believed in the concept of the lithograph as a multiple drawing.[2] He maintained that "lithography reveals the artist in his true strength as a draughtsman and colourist – for the line comes straight from his pencil."[3] *Gants de suède* is an excellent example of Whistler's draughtsmanship.

The Studio magazine, which included artist's lithographs from the time of its first appearance in 1893, did much to stimulate the revival of artistic lithography in England. Whistler watched its progress with great interest from the other side of the Channel. He wrote to Way on 12 September 1893, "Perhaps we may do something for 'The Studio' – you tell me it is 'catching on'."[4] He appointed Tom Way his agent in dealing with the *Studio* and other magazines.

Whistler's fee for the inclusion of lithographs in magazines began at ten guineas and gradually doubled. The editor of *The Studio*, Gleeson White, offered ten pounds sterling for *Gants de suède* on condition that fifty extra impressions be included. Whistler was horrified, and refused to allow him any proofs beyond those needed in the publication.[5] In January 1894, Whistler authorised Way to print the exact number required for the magazine.[6]

Whenever he allowed his lithographs to appear in journals, Whistler instructed Way to transfer the image to a second stone, and keep the master stone for his own proofs. The lithographs that appeared in *The Studio* were always printed on white wove paper, with *The Studio* blind stamp clearly impressed in them.

1 Andrew McLaren Young, Margaret MacDonald, Robin Spencer and Hamish Miles, *The Paintings of James McNeill Whistler* (New Haven and London: Yale University Press, 1980), p. 175, no. 395.

2 I am indebted to Douglas Druick for this information.

3 Whistler to Marcus Huish (1895), GUL BP 11 c/36.

4 Whistler to Way, 12 September 1893, LC PC.

5 Whistler to Gleeson White, December 1893, BP 11 Res 18e/43-45.

6 Whistler to Way, January 18 1894, LC PC.

24 *Gants de suède*, 1890

25 *The Draped Figure Seated*, 1893

25 *The Draped Figure Seated*
from *L'Estampe Originale* 1893
W. 46, L. 74
Transfer lithograph on old laid paper
27.4 x 20.9 cm (sheet)
Ex. coll. Rosalind Birnie Philip
(round stamp, brown, *verso*) not in Lugt
Gift of Touche Ross, 1978
Acc. no. 77/166

One of the loveliest of the black-and-white Tanagra subjects, *The Draped Figure Seated* was made in Whistler's Paris studio. He was very interested in capturing the translucent properties of the drapery, which partly reveal and partly conceal the form beneath.

Whistler was delighted with the rich tonal effects he had achieved using paper stumps with sauce made from chalk in solution. He wrote to Way in 1893, "The little sitting figure in drapery I am immensely pleased with.... Do you see I am getting to use the stump just like a brush – and the work is beginning to have the mystery in execution of a painting."[1] He swore the printer to secrecy with the injunction, "you are not to talk to everyone or anyone about this stump phase of the lithograph that I am developing!.... That is *mine* you know – and I don't want all the busy lot that you have got about you just now, to get bedeviling with it before I have established the success and beauty of the thing."[2]

On 12 November 1893, Whistler informed Way that André Marty, editor and publisher of portfolios of lithographs entitled *L'Estampe originale*, was on his way to London from Paris to select a work for inclusion. He wrote, "as I shall be in the same box with the others, and as Puvis de Chavannes, Bracquemond, Fantin, and the rest are going to be in it – I have promised.... [L]et us be very swell among them all!"[3] The *Draped Figure Seated* was selected, and an edition of 100 impressions was printed from a second stone at Whistler's instructions.[4] Goulding printed fifteen posthumous impressions of which this is one. Miss Birnie Philip identified the Goulding impressions by stamping them on the verso in brown ink, using a circular stamp containing her initials.[5]

1 Whistler to Way, 21 November 1893, GUL BP 11 Res 18e/30.

2 Whistler to Way, 3 October 1893, GUL BP 11 Res 18e/21.

3 Whistler to Way, 12 November 1893, GUL BP 11 Res. 18. e/29.

4 Whistler to Way, 28 November 1893, GUL BP Res 18e/33.

5 Elizabeth Robins and Joseph Pennell, *The Whistler Journal* (Philadelphia: J.B. Lippincott Co., 1921), p. 149.

26 *A Draped Model Standing Beside a Sofa*
L. 187 (not in Way)
Transfer lithograph on old laid paper
taken from a Greek concordance
38.1 x 23.6 cm (sheet)
Ex. coll. Rosalind Birnie Philip
Gift of Touche Ross, 1978
Acc. no. 77/164

One of the subjects that reappeared in Whistler's late lithographs was the "Tanagra" theme. It first entered his work in 1865 when he fell under the influence of Albert Moore (1841-1893), whose Grecian beauties, timeless in their own right, were inspired by the Elgin Marbles. What appealed to Whistler was not their classicism *per se*, but the fact that, unlike the work of other adherents of the Greek revival, the draped women of Moore were allegories of beauty devoid of subject-matter or narrative content.

Whistler had always admired Greek sculpture. Soon after his arrival in Paris in 1855, he went to the Louvre to see the Venus de Milo, which he thought the most perfect thing ever made. Although he abandoned his classical training while under the influence of Courbet and Realism, it resurfaced after his meeting with Moore and the Ingres retro-

26 *A Draped Model Standing Beside a Sofa*

spective exhibition held in Paris in 1867. He began to look once again at the art of Greece, but at a more intimate variety than the Venus.

At this time, the first small terracotta figurines were being unearthed near Tanagra in Greece. During the early 1860s, Alexander Ionides, a Greek shipping magnate, began to form an outstanding collection. Whistler, who was a friend of the Ionides' sons, spent a lot of time at their home at Tulse Hill in London, and saw the figurines as they arrived. He was very taken by their beauty, delicacy and charm. They were almost all standing female figures draped in a thin undergarment, a chiton, and a mantle or himation, which partly concealed, and partly revealed, the form beneath.

At the same time, Whistler had become one of the earliest collectors of the art of Japan, which first became available on the Paris market in 1862. He enthusiastically accumulated Japanese prints, kimonos, blue and white china, and furnishings, and saw in the art of Japan an aesthetic perfection rivalling that of Greece.

Together with Albert Moore, Whistler created a strange hybrid of Greek and Japanese elements to arrive at a concept of ideal beauty. In the "Ten O'Clock" lecture of 1888 he declared, "The story of the beautiful is already complete, hewn in the marbles of the Parthenon – and broidered, with the birds, upon the fan of Hokusai – at the foot of Fusiyama."[1] After exploring this theme in painting during the late 1860s, Whistler abandoned it, afraid that his work would be confused with that of Moore. He returned to it in the lithographs of 1890, at which time he was helping with the sale of the Ionides Tanagras. In this lithograph, the female nude is loosely draped in one of the kimonos from Whistler's collection.

A Draped Model is closely related to Whistler's work in pastel, and can be compared to A Masked Woman and The Arabian at the Hunterian Art Gallery at Glasgow University.[2] The model may be Hetty Pettigrew who, in The Arabian, reclines semi-nude on the same sofa, draped with a Japanese kimono. If so, the lithograph was probably made in London before Whistler's move to Paris in 1892. Unknown to Thomas Way, and not included in his catalogue raisonné of Whistler's lithographs, it appears to have been transferred to stone, but not printed, prior to Whistler's death, and was probably listed as "Nude with a Japanese Robe" among the "untried drawings" inherited by Rosalind Birnie Philip. The small posthumous edition was printed by Goulding.[3] This impression was printed on a curious piece of old laid paper torn from a Greek concordance. Whistler appears to have had a whole concordance, as there are a number of etchings and lithographs printed on similar sheet of paper. Handwriting or mildew marks never bothered Whistler, as they did Way: he had great affection for the patina of age.

1 Whistler, "Mr. Whistler's 'Ten O'Clock'", in The Gentle Art of Making Enemies, p. 159.

2 See Margaret MacDonald, Whistler Pastels (Glasgow: The Hunterian Art Gallery, 1984), no. 52, pls. 5 and 6.

3 See Susan Hobbs and Nesta Spink, Lithographs of James McNeill Whistler (Washington: Smithsonian Institution, 1982), note 40, p. 59.

27   *Draped Figure Reclining* c. 1893
W. 156, L. 194
Six-colour transfer lithograph on *japon mince*
20.8 x 31.8 cm (sheet)
Signed in pencil with the butterfly
Ex. colls. A.W. Scholle (L.2923a);
Emma Regina Martin (initials, *verso*), and an anonymous collector's mark (not in Lugt)
Gift of Esther and Arthur Gelber, 1981
Acc. no. 80/101

Whistler became interested in colour lithography around 1891, when he conceived a scheme for producing lithographs of his pastels.[1] T.R. Way set to work to discover a method for doing this, and made facsimile drawings of Whistler's pastels on transfer paper, which he printed successfully on brown paper. While Way was trying to come to grips with the problem of colour printing, Whistler began to experiment at the printer Belfont's in Paris, where technical knowledge was much more advanced. Joseph Pennell saw him there in May 1892, planning a series of colour lithographs.[2]

Whistler abhorred the overprinting of colours used in commercial chromolithography, and wanted to keep his colours clear like the colours in a Japanese woodcut, juxtaposing colour areas like stones in a mosaic.[3] He developed a method of printing each colour separately by making a master drawing on paper and having as many proofs pulled on transfer paper as he wanted colours. After scraping away the areas not to be coloured, he had the drawings on transfer paper transferred to as many stones as there were colours to be printed. These were then printed in succession. The precise registration of colours in printing was effected by means of four marks placed in the centre of each side of the sheet.

His most complex colour lithograph was *Draped Figure Reclining*. In it, Whistler combined the Greek and Japanese elements that were the twin poles of his aesthetic (see no. 26). It may have been inspired in part by such rare reclining Tanagras as *An Interesting Group*, from the Ionides collection. The delicate colouring used in the lithograph recalls the terracotta body of the Tanagras, and the traces of pigment that remain on some of them.

27   *Draped Figure Reclining*, c. 1893
See colour plate on page 6

Draped Figure was to have been printed in Paris by Belfont and published by William Heinemann in *Songs on Stone*. The idea for this portfolio dates from 1891; three years later, on 11 May 1894, Heinemann sent Whistler a draft contract.[4] However, Belfont's shop suddenly closed later that year, and both printer and stones disappeared.

While the print cannot be dated absolutely, it seems likely that this is the lithograph referred to in a letter to David Croal Thomson of 8 September 1894, which accompanied an impression of a colour lithograph referred to as "*la belle dame paresseuse*." Whistler pointed out in the letter that "this sort of lithograph ceases to be 'chromo'."[5]

Whistler stood by the press and ground the colours. Only a small number of proofs were pulled, no two alike. This is one of the most beautiful: the colours are very subtly modulated, and the print is printed on silky, sensuous Japanese paper.

1 Alan Cole's Diary, 12 October 1891, LC PC.

2 Pennell, *Life*, vol. 2, pp. 35-36.

3 Pennell, "Whistler as Etcher and Lithographer," typescript, LC PC.

4 There was considerable correspondence between Heinemann and Whistler in 1891 (BP H. 179-184, GUL). The matter picks up again in 1894. See Heinemann to Whistler, 11 May 1894. On this same date, 1894, William Rothenstein bore word that under no circumstances would Whistler do the lithographs. See Heinemann to Whistler, 11 May 1894, BP H. 187, GUL.

5 Whistler to P.C. Thomson, 8 September 1894, LC PC. Whistler not infrequently changed the titles of his lithographs. This title was subsequently attached to a black-and-white lithograph, W. 62, 1894.

28 *Nursemaids – Les Bonnes de Luxembourg*, 1894
W. 48, L. 79
Transfer lithograph on wove paper
31.3 x 21.7 cm (sheet)
Purchase, 1973
Acc. no. 73/59

Whistler made this print on 8 February 1894, in the garden terrace that surrounds the Luxembourg Palace, Paris, then a museum of contemporary French art.[1] The Luxembourg had special significance for Whistler. As an art student he had copied paintings there, and in November 1891 the museum purchased his *Arrangement in Grey and Black: Portrait of the Painter's Mother* (Y. 101). This meant a very great deal to him. The painting was later transferred, along with the rest of the Luxembourg collection, to the Louvre.

The gardens were just up the street from Whistler's studio at 186 rue Notre-Dame-des-Champs, and he must have strolled through them regularly with copper plates and transfer paper. This lithograph of children with their nurses recalls the etchings made at Gray's Inn, London, in 1866-68 (no. 19), in which Whistler also played with pattern and ground. The disposition of the figures on the sheet recalls the page-layout of Hokusai's *Manga*, which he would have

28 *Nursemaids – Les Bonnes de Luxembourg*, 1894

known well. In the loose drawing of the figures, he very effectively suggested motion.

Whistler made the lithograph specifically for publication in the *Art Journal* and sent it to London the day after it was drawn for transfer to the stone.[2] Proofs were in Paris by February 13, at which time he wrote to Way that the figures of the boy, nurse and child required "lightening."[3] The lithograph was published two years later, in 1896.

1 Whistler to Way, 9 February 1894, Freer, 125.

2 Whistler to Way, 9 February 1894, GUL BP 11 Res 18e/48.

3 Whistler to Way, 13 February 1894, GUL BP 11 Res 18e/49.

29 *Long Gallery, Louvre* from *The Studio* 1894
W. 52, L. 83
Transfer lithograph on wove paper
29.8 x 21.0 cm (sheet)
Gallery Purchase, 1923
Acc. no. 739

Whistler had a deep affection for the Louvre, where he spent hours as a student studying the history of art and copying paintings, just like the artist in the middle distance of this print. The Long Gallery looks very much the same today,

30 *La Belle Jardinière*, 1894

although the paintings are not as densely hung.

When Whistler and his wife moved to Paris in 1892, they settled on the rue du Bac on the Left Bank, a ten-minute walk from the Louvre. There can be little doubt that he continued to haunt the museum in the last phase of his career. In his will, he offered to leave to the Louvre his wife's collection of garnets, together with his silver and china, on two conditions: that it be "gathered together in one and displayed as the Beatrice Whistler Collection," and that "in the same room shall be hung proofs of my wife's exquisite etchings."[1]

On 30 July 1894, Whistler wrote to Way, "Mr. Gleeson White can have this."[2] The print was published in *The Studio* magazine in 1894.

1 James McNeill Whistler, Last Will and Testament, London, Public Records Office. Whistler left Rosalind Birnie Philip life interest, and expressed a desire, "but not so as in any way to control or bind her", that she give these items to the Louvre. She gave them to Glasgow University.

2 Whistler to Way, 30 July 1894, GUL BP 11 Res 18e/62.

29 *Long Gallery, Louvre,* 1894

30 *La Belle Jardinière* 1894
W. 63, L. 94
Transfer lithograph on old laid paper
32.4 x 20.5 cm (sheet)
Ex. coll. Rosalind Birnie Philip
(square stamp, brown, *verso*) not in Lugt
Gift of Touche Ross, 1978
Acc. no. 77/170

The Whistlers acquired their apartment at 110 rue du Bac in Paris in 1892, and moved in after extensive redecorating in 1893. They were extremely happy there, and in 1894 Whistler made many transfer lithographs – little slices of life with the disarming simplicity of a snapshot. As such, they are very much in tune with the *intimiste* lithographs of Edmond Vuillard and Pierre Bonnard. In them we see Mrs. Whistler in the garden and salon, and the friends and relatives who came to visit. The garden gave the Whistlers and their guests great pleasure. They entertained in it on Sunday, when the weather was nice, and enjoyed listening to the monks chanting in the monastery garden on the other side of the wall.

After receiving proofs of this lithograph, Whistler wrote to Way, "Really La Belle Jardinière is delightful."[1] He was very pleased with the way in which the delicate use of stump resembled charcoal in the dark passages, giving them the "*fusain*" look he liked. The sparkle and crispness of this impression pulled by Way is exceptional, and can be used as a standard against which to judge other impressions of Whistler's lithographs.

Miss Birnie Philip stamped the impressions pulled by Way with a brown stamp bearing her initials "R.B.P." in a square border.[2]

1 Whistler to T.R. Way, 18 September 1894, BP 11 Res 18e/65.

2 See Pennell, *Whistler Journal*, p. 149.

31 *The Duet* 1894
W. 64, L. 95
Transfer lithograph on modern laid paper
33.2 x 19.9 cm (sheet)
Inscr. "G" by the printer Charles Goulding,
pencil, lower right corner
Ex. coll. Rosalind Birnie Philip
Gift of Touche Ross, 1978
Acc. no. 77/169

The theme of middle-class domestic genre entered Whistler's work during his early Realist period, when he was influenced by the seventeenth-century Dutch tradition and was deliberately looking for subjects from modern life. His first Salon submission, *At the Piano*, of 1858-9 (Y. 24), showed Deborah Haden playing while her daughter, Annie, listened. The painting was rejected, and hung instead at François Bonvin's "*atelier flamand*" where it was admired by Courbet. This marked the beginning of Whistler's career as a painter, and his association with the leaders of the Realist movement.

Whistler returned to the musical theme in the lithograph *The Duet*, which shows Beatrice with her sister Ethel Whibley at the piano in the salon at the rue de Bac. The close harmony that existed between the sisters is symbolically underlined, as they appear to be physically united in the shadowed interior.

In the early painting, Whistler sought the timeless quality found in the seventeenth-century Dutch interiors of Gerard Ter Borch (1617-1681). In the lithograph, he was concerned instead with a transient, momentary glimpse of domestic life. This is expressed in the elusive and discontinuous line of the transfer lithograph, which has a tentative and fragile appearance.

Whistler was not terribly happy with the quality of the transfer, and wrote to Way on 14 September 1894, "The Duet…I don't think so highly of."[1] He may have retouched this image when he returned to London in 1895.[2] He attempted a second version, *The Duet No. 2*, 1894 (W. 65), which was weak, and ultimately destroyed. This impression was printed by Goulding, and bears his cypher.

1 Whistler to Way, 14 September 1894, LC PC.

2 Hobbs and Spink, *Lithographs of James McNeill Whistler* p. 68, note 69.

32   *La robe rouge* from *The Studio* 1894
W. 68, L. 96
Transfer lithograph on wove paper
28.3 x 20.0 cm
Gallery Purchase, 1923
Acc. no. 740

This lithograph shows Beatrice Whistler wearing a red dress, resting in the parlour at the rue du Bac. Whistler considered that he had successfully suggested the colour of her dress.[1]

On 1 October 1894, Whistler wrote to T.R. Way to say that he was thinking of retouching the drawing on the stone.[2] The print was published in the *Studio* magazine in 1894.

1 Way, *Memories*, p. 95.

2 Whistler to Way, 1 October 1894, GUL BP 11 Res 18e/68.

32 *La robe rouge*, 1894

31 *The Duet*, 1894

33 *The Sisters* 1894
W. 71a II/II, L. 106
Transfer lithograph on old laid paper
19.8 x 29.4 cm (sheet)
Ex. coll. Rosalind Birnie Philip
(square stamp, brown, *verso*)
Gift of Touche Ross, 1978
Acc. no. 77/165

The two Philip sisters, Beatrice and Ethel, were once again fused into a double portrait in this work, which was made in the parlour at the rue du Bac. Whistler appears to have been principally interested in silhouette, and flattened the figures in a style derived from Japanese wood block prints.

Beatrice encouraged Whistler's pursuit of lithography, despite the fact that it brought few financial rewards. According to Tom Way, "Mrs. Whistler showed the very greatest interest in the matter, as though she felt it offered him a field where he might surpass his reputation in any other of his works."[1] She and members of her family predominate as subjects in the lithographs of 1894.

This impression was pulled by Way.

1 Way, *Memories*, p. 91.

33 *The Sisters*, 1894

34 *La fruitière de la rue de Grenelle* 1894
W. 70, L. 98
Transfer lithograph on old laid paper
29.1 x 20.2 cm (sheet)
Ex. coll. Rosalind Birnie Philip
Gift of Touche Ross, 1978
Acc. no. 77/163

One of Whistler's finest lithographs, *La fruitière de la rue de Grenelle* was apparently the first of the series of prints devoted to Paris shops.[1] The subject can be seen as a lithographic variation on the etched London shopfronts of 1884-88 and the Paris shopfronts of 1892-93.

The rue de Grenelle runs off the rue du Bac, and it is likely that the fruit shop was just around the corner from the apartment. Whistler's careful selection of details from the façade, to fit his oriental sense of selectivity, balance and

placement, is very evident in this work.

Whistler wrote to Way asking for proofs on 1 October 1894, asking him to "let them be full and rich."[2]

1 Joseph Pennell, *The Walter H. Jessup Collection of Lithographs by Whistler* (New York: The Anderson Galleries, 1919), p. 65.

2 Whistler to T.R. Way, 1 October 1894, GUL BP 11 Res 18e/68.

35 *The Smith's Yard* from *The Studio* 1895
W. 88, L. 126
Transfer lithograph on wove paper
18.5 x 15.8 cm
Gallery Purchase, 1923
Acc. no. 741

The Smith's Yard was made in the picturesque seaside town of Lyme Regis in Devon, where Whistler took Beatrice for her health on 15 September 1895. She returned to London late in October, and he stayed on until the end of November to complete his work. Whistler made ten lithographs and two paintings at the smithy of Samuel Edward Govier (1855-1934).[1] His interest in this subject can be traced back to his drypoint *The Forge* of 1861 (no. 10), and ultimately to his admiration for the blacksmiths of Delacroix and Bonvin.

Whistler liked this work and could not understand why the New York dealer Edward Kennedy did not. He wrote to him on 14 March 1896 that this was one of the two "most remarkable among the new lithographs – the most per-

35 *The Smith's Yard*, 1895

34 *La fruitière de la rue de Grenelle*, 1894

sonal...most brilliant things in the whole collection... prime favorites of all the would-be connoisseurs."[2]

The Smith's Yard was published in *The Studio* magazine in 1895.

1 Young, MacDonald, Spencer and Miles, *The Paintings of James McNeill Whistler*, vol. 2, no. 450, p. 199.

2 Whistler to Edward Kennedy, 14 March 1896, LC PC.

36 *The Blacksmith* 1895
W. 90 II/II, L. 128
Transfer lithograph on old laid paper
28.9 x 20.3 cm (sheet)
Ex. coll. Rosalind Birnie Philip
(round stamp, brown, *verso*)
Gift of Touche Ross, 1978
Acc. no. 77/171

This study of the blacksmith Samuel Edward Govier (1855-1934), the subject of Whistler's portrait painting, *The Master Smith of Lyme Regis* (Y. 450), was made between mid-September and the end of November 1895, while Whistler was staying in Lyme Regis.[1]

Whistler clearly welcomed the opportunity afforded by the forge to play with chiaroscuro effects. He finished the lithograph in London, and had Tom Way stand in the same pose so that he could strengthen the drawing.[2] The likeness to the blacksmith remained unchanged. In 1914, the etcher Muirhead Bone went to visit Lyme Regis, and made a "Whistler pilgrimage" through the town. He found the blacksmith "who looked like the lithograph and painting, and who," he reported, "is as handsome as ever."[3]

In this work, Whistler continued to play with the theme of the figure silhouetted in a doorway which had entered his work in 1858 (no. 3).

This impression was printed by Goulding.

1 Young, MacDonald, Spencer and Miles, *The Paintings of James McNeill Whistler*, vol. 2, no. 450, p. 199.

2 Way, *Memories*, p. 117.

3 Pennell, *Whistler Journal*, pp. 56-57.

37 *The Doctor* from the *Pageant* 1894
W. 78, L. 117
Transfer lithograph on wove paper
25.3 x 18.4 cm (sheet)
Gift of Mr. and Mrs. Ralph Presgrave, 1976
Acc. no. 76/240

William Whistler, Whistler's younger brother, was born in 1836 in Lowell, Massachusetts. After studying medicine in Philadelphia, he distinguished himself as a surgeon and soldier attached to the Confederate army during the American Civil War. Following the War, he settled in London, where he carried on a practice from his home on Wimpole Street. Whistler could always count on his brother and sister-in-law's sympathetic support, and stayed with them after his return to London from Venice.

36 *The Blacksmith*, 1895   37 *The Doctor*, 1894

Tom Way described the doctor as follows: "his manner was slow and sedate, and entirely opposed to any form of push and advertisement; as a result, while he was at one time, perhaps, the leading laryngologist in London, he failed to reap any considerable pecuniary benefit from his skill."[1] Way maintained that Whistler had a "real childlike faith in his brother's skill as a physician, and used to say that if anything happened to the Doctor, he himself would soon die, as he looked after him so carefully, and that he was a 'great magician' in medicine."

Whistler made this portrait of the Doctor when he came to Paris to consult on Beatrice's condition in 1894. The visit was traumatic, for William diagnosed cancer and stopped an obscure French doctor from proceeding with a planned operation. Whistler subsequently took Beatrice on a futile search for more optimistic medical opinions in London. Mrs. Whistler apparently accepted the Doctor's verdict and did not make a secret of it, which greatly upset Whistler. The diagnosis, which Whistler refused to accept, finally led to a terrible quarrel, and Whistler broke off relations with his brother.

It is probably because of its sad association that Whistler neglected to have the portrait transferred to stone while it was still fresh. He wrote to Way on 2 November 1894, "I don't know at all about the Doctor's portraits. The fact is I had thrown them aside and had given up all thought of having them ever printed – it was Mrs. Whistler who had a better opinion of them and sent them on to you – so now we will see!"[2] The proofs were back in Paris two days later,

for Whistler wrote on 4 November, "This is really fine. I wish I had sent it to you when quite *fresh*. I like the proofs with the sharp bright black lines in the coat."[3]

The rift between Whistler and the Doctor survived Mrs. Whistler's death: William heard of it by accident while dining at the Savoy. The quarrel so preyed on him that it "drove him to the 'unfortunate habits' which caused his death." When he fell ill, Whistler rushed over to see him in response to a plea from his wife.[4] Apparently the Doctor told Whistler that he had a heart condition, but that he would outlive him, which he did.

On 15 July 1895, Way wrote to tell Whistler that Charles Shannon had been made editor of a new publication, and wanted to publish a lithograph. On 22 July Whistler wrote back to say that Mr. Shannon was "allowed to have this for his new magazine under the usual conditions, making a transfer of course, and keeping the original stone untouched for my proofs."[5]

1 Way, *Memories*, pp. 60-61.

2 Whistler to Way, 2 November 1894, GUL BP 11 Res 18e/70.

3 Whistler to Way, 4 November 1894, GUL BP 11 Res 18e/71.

4 Pennell, *Whistler Journal*, p. 253.

5 Whistler to Way, 22 July 1895, BP 11 Res. 18e/76.

fig. 9, Dr. William Whistler.
Glasgow University Library, Birnie Philip Bequest.

38 *Firelight: Joseph Pennell* 1896
W. 104, L. 152
Transfer lithograph on *simile japon*
28.7 x 21.9 cm (sheet)
Ex. coll. Rosalind Birnie Philip
(square stamp, brown, *verso*)
Gift of Touche Ross, 1978
Acc. no. 77/112

It was in 1893 that Joseph Pennell (nos. 54 and 55) got to know Whistler, and assisted with the printing of the Paris etchings. He and his wife, Elizabeth Robins, were invited frequently to the rue du Bac and became intimate friends during Beatrice Whistler's last illness. Pennell later recalled how "All the while a shadow was approaching, and at last it touched him – his wife's illness – and the apartment in Paris was closed and the studio was shut up, and he started on those pilgrimages to find her lost health that ended only with her death. And during her illness at the Savoy, where he was staying, he would come to us in Buckingham Street. And it was then that he made the lithographs."[1]

The Pennells were at home to their friends on Thursday evenings; however, the possibility of a chance encounter with Whistler scared many of their regular guests away. Their Thursday nights became "Whistler nights": they would hear "the memorable and unmistakeable knock and ring at our front door…rousing the whole house" when he arrived; then they would talk, Whistler always "full of reminiscences, of comment, of criticism, of friendliness, his talk none the less stimulating and splendid because, at his request, the cuff or note-book was always ready."[2] It was at this time that the Pennells began to collect material for their two-volume biography of Whistler.

In making this lithograph, which took about an hour, Whistler apparently sat on the floor, his paper lit by flickering firelight.[3] His primary concern was not the subject, but the distortion of the human form seen in firelight, and the shadows it cast on the wall. His interest in *chiaroscuro* compositions lit from within recalls his early etching, *The Music Room*, of 1858 (no. 4).

This impression was pulled by Way.

1 Joseph Pennell, *The Adventures of an Illustrator* (Boston, Little, Brown and Co., 1925), p. 242.

2 Elizabeth Pennell, *Nights: Rome, Venice in the Aesthetic Eighties, London, Paris in the Fighting Nineties* (London, 1916), pp. 216-220.

3 Pennell, *The Walter H. Jessup Collection of Lithographs by Whistler* p. 91.

38 *Firelight: Joseph Pennell*, 1896

39 *Walter Sickert* 1895
W. 104, L. 152
Transfer lithograph on wove paper
31.8 x 20.2 cm (sheet)
Ex. coll. Rosalind Birnie Philip
Gift of Touche Ross, 1978
Acc. no. 77/167

Like Pennell, Walter Sickert (no. 61) was very close to Whistler immediately prior to Mrs. Whistler's death. It was a very difficult time for Whistler, as he tried desperately to cling to his hopes for her recovery, while knowing that the end was inevitable. The winter and spring of 1895-96 must have been the longest of his life.

Whistler made this lithograph of Sickert by firelight at the Pennell's flat on Buckingham Street, possibly as a pendant to the study of Pennell (no. 38). This portrait, over which the flames dance, suggests the creative brilliance of Whistler's most talented "follower," and the one whom he was to reject so callously. Whistler's interest in immortalizing his "followers" recalls his early drypoints of artist friends in Paris of 1859 (no. 9).

39 *Walter Sickert*, 1895

40 *Needlework* 1896
W. 113, L. 161
Transfer lithograph on wove paper
31.9 x 20.2 cm (sheet)
Ex. coll. Rosalind Birnie Philip
Gift of Touche Ross, 1978
Acc. no. 77/168

From January to April 1896, Whistler and his wife lived in the Savoy Hotel in London in a room overlooking the Thames. Beatrice was often attended during this period by her youngest sister, Rosalind Birnie Philip, who must have sat with Whistler for hours by the bedside. The closeness that developed between Whistler and Rosalind, then aged twenty-three, was very important to him after his wife's death on 10 May 1896. Two weeks later he adopted Rosalind as his ward and made her his executrix. She was his constant companion until his death in 1903, carrying out his commissions, running his household, and nursing him during his final illness.[1] She ultimately left the contents of Whistler's estate to Glasgow University.

Needlework is one of the most satisfying and sensitive of Whistler's portrait lithographs. It appears to have been executed by firelight; the composed figure is enlivened by the shadows cast on the wall, which help to integrate her with the environment.

1 See Kate Donnelly and Nigel Thorp, *Whistlers and Further Family* (Glasgow: Glasgow University Library, 1980), p. 25.

40 *Needlework*, 1896

41 *Savoy Pigeons* from *The Studio* 1896
W. 118, L. 164
Transfer lithograph on laid paper
29.2 x 20.6 cm (sheet)
Gallery Purchase, 1923
Acc. no. 738

The Savoy Hotel, London, where Whistler and his wife took up residence in the winter and spring of 1896, held fond memories, for it was in the Savoy Theatre that he had delivered his "Ten O'Clock" lecture in 1888. The hotel was situated close to T.R. Way's printing establishment on Wellington Street in the Strand, and overlooked the Victoria Embankment, providing Whistler with a superb view of the Thames and the hansom cabs which he referred to as the "gondolas of London."[1] Whistler made a number of lithographs from the window, while sitting with his wife during the last months of her illness. He made this view looking toward Charing Cross Railway Bridge, Big Ben and the Houses of Parliament. He was pleased with it and wrote to the New York dealer Edward Kennedy, "I don't see how you can help liking some of the things I have done out of the windows overlooking the river!"[2] This understated

vignette is very much the equivalent in lithography of Whistler's etched "notes" of the 1880s.

According to T.R. Way, lithography was the one form of work that Whistler seemed able to get on with at this time, and he always wanted proofs of his latest drawings as quickly as possible in order to show Beatrice.[3] On 7 April 1896, Whistler wrote to the painter Frederick Sandys to inform him that they were moving to Hampstead the next day: "My wife, you may have heard, has for a long time been suffering, and so we have gone from place to place and from doctor to medical imposter. But now I am happy to say that things are brighter.... Like yourself I have been unable to do work and at last learned that health is everything."[4] Despite Whistler's desperate optimism, Beatrice died in Hampstead on 10 May 1896. Whistler never picked up the lithographic chalk again.

1 Way, *Memories*, p. 128.

2 Whistler to Edward Kennedy, 25 March 1896, LC PC.

3 Way, *Memories*, p. 92.

4 Whistler to Anthony Frederick Augustus Sandys, 8 April 1896, LC PC.

41 *Savoy Pigeons*, 1896

THE WHISTLER CIRCLE

42 Clifford Addams
American (1876-1942)
Admiral's House in Amsterdam 1902/1920/1924
Drypoint on laid paper
25.9 x 18.5 cm (imp.)
Gift of the Canadian National Exhibition, 1966
Acc. no. 215

Clifford Addams was born in Woodbury, New Jersey. After studies in Philadelphia, he went on to apprentice in architecture. In 1899, at the age of twenty-three, he won a scholarship at the Pennsylvania Academy of Fine Arts, which enabled him to study painting in Paris. In November, when his scholarship money ran out, Addams entered Whistler's Académie Carmen. He was interviewed by Miss Inez Bate, a young woman from a comfortable English family, who had enrolled at the Academy when it was founded. Whistler admired her work and asked her to be his "*massière*", or chief woman student. In 1899 he invited her to become his apprentice for a period of five years.

On 19 July 1900, Clifford Addams and Inez Bate were married. Addams was taken on by Whistler as an apprentice, and learnt Whistler's methods through his wife and his contact with Whistler. He wrote, "I have been able to comprehend sufficiently enough to tell you that [Whistler's] system or craft has a depth and beauty undreamed of by me, and which I believe, once mastered, would be consid-

ered a way of working of the old Masters."[1]

There is no evidence to suggest that Addams tried etching before meeting Whistler in Paris. His earliest plates date from 1902; in that year he began *The Admiral's House, Amsterdam*, which he signed in the plate "*élève de Whistler*". In his choice of venue, subject matter and style, Addams shows his awareness of Whistler's Amsterdam etchings of 1888 (no. 21). The delicacy of the hatching and the beauty of the reflections recall Whistler's *Square House, Amsterdam* (K. 404). The approach to the subject is less frontal than Whistler's, and the unfinished row of houses leading into the picture space recall Whistler's etching *Wych Street* (K. 159), of 1877. In addition to etching in Amsterdam, Addams also worked at different times in his life in Dordrecht, London and Venice, following in Whistler's footsteps.

After the Académie Carmen was closed in April 1901, the Addamses remained in Paris where they had their first child, Dianne, who became Whistler's goddaughter. They went for holidays to Dieppe, Dordrecht and Amsterdam, cities in which Whistler liked to sketch and etch. After Whistler returned to London from Corsica in 1902, the Addams moved there and remained devoted friends, visiting him almost daily until his death in 1903.

While Inez was highly organized, Clifford was lively and uninhibited.[2] He apparently found both Whistler's capricious methods and the extraordinary amount of freedom offered by the Académie Carmen to his liking. In 1920 he deserted his wife and four children and returned to America, where he achieved a degree of artistic fame and lived for the rest of his life in Washington Square, Greenwich Village.

1 See Dawn Addams' foreward to Meg Hausberg, *Addams: Etchings and Drypoints* (London: Lott and Gerrish Ltd., 1984).

2 Robert H. Getscher, *The Stamp of Whistler* (Oberlin: Allen Memorial Art Museum, 1977), p. 268.

43 John Taylor Arms
American (1887-1953)
Lace, Place Victor Hugo, Lisieux 1919
A. 18 26/50
Etching in warm black ink on Japanese paper
17.8 x 24.1 cm (imp.)
Signed and dated in the margin below plate right "John Taylor Arms, 1919"
Gift of the Canadian National Exhibition, 1966
Acc. no. 108

Arms was born in Washington in 1887. He studied architecture at the Massachusetts Institute of Technology and draughtsmanship under Désiré Déspradelle, a graduate of the École des Beaux-Arts in Paris. It was through the work of one of Whistler's admirers, the etcher Ernest S. Lumsden, author of *The Art of Etching* (1924), that Arms became interested in etching. He purchased a print by Whistler which was the beginning of a collection of etchings that would ultimately number 5,000 sheets.

After serving in the U.S. Navy during World War I, Arms decided to devote himself to etching in 1919. It was in that

42 Addams, *Admiral's House in Amsterdam*, 1902/1920/1924

43 Arms, *Lace, Place Victor Hugo, Lisieux*, 1919

year that he made the plate *Lace, Place Victor Hugo, Lisieux*. Given his training as an architect, and the strong emotional response that he felt throughout his life towards the Gothic, it is not surprising to find the "quaint half-timbered houses that line the streets of the '*ancien quartier*' of Lisieux" as the focal point of his first etchings.[1]

This plate shows the unmistakable influence of Whistler's London streetscapes of the 1880s. The composition employs the same division of space, with the road occupying the foreground and the buildings the middle ground. The diagonal approach, and the emphasis on the three-dimensional nature of the structures, are reminiscent of Whistler's earlier etching, *The "Adam and Eve," Old Chelsea* (no. 11), dated 1879. The concept and title recall Whistler's Amsterdam etching, *The Embroidered Curtain*, which Mansfield maintained should be called "The Lace Curtain."[2]

Arms showed himself to be selective while under the influence of Whistler. Rather than omitting detail, the mature Arms left nothing to the imagination. He was aware of the fact that this was a weakness, for he stated that "an etcher must be able to eliminate unessentials," and added, "It is the hardest thing I have to do."[3] Like Whistler, he also etched in Paris and Venice.

This impression was pulled by Frederick Reynolds, one of several printers who worked for Arms.

1 S. William Pelletier, "John Taylor Arms: An American Medievalist", *The Georgia Review* 33 (Winter 1976): 912.

2 Howard Mansfield, *Whistler in Belgium and Holland* (New York: Knoedler and Co., n.d.), p. 19.

3 Quoted by S. William Pelletier in "John Taylor Arms: An Evaluation", *Print Review* 14 (Winter 1981): 18-19, from "Etching Retrospective Held by Arms", *Art Digest* (15 March 1935): 22.

44   Clarence Gagnon
Canadian (1881-1942)
Moonlight, Venice 1906
5/30
Warm black ink with plate tone on Japanese paper
16.9 x 10.0 cm (imp.)
Signed and dated in pencil "Clarence A. Gagnon '06"
Bequest of Frank Darling, 1923
Acc. no. 877

Gagnon began his artistic career in Montreal as a student of William Brymner (1855-1925) at the Art Association of Montreal.[1] He took up etching in 1904 and made a few early plates which show the influence of the Barbizon and Hague schools, then popular with Montreal collectors. The department store-owner James Morgan offered to pay for his schooling in Paris if he would supply twelve pictures a year for display and sale in Morgan's art gallery. Gagnon arrived in Paris in January 1904. He entered the Académie Julian and made excursions to Spain to see the paintings of Velasquez. When, in 1905 and 1906, his etchings were included in the Salon des Artistes français, the critic for the *Gazette des Beaux-Arts* identified him as one of a group of "*charmants artistes continuant la tradition whistlerienne*".[2]

Gagnon made two trips to Venice in 1905 and 1906, producing ten plates, of which only eight are known today.

44 Gagnon, *Moonlight, Venice*, 1906

Moonlight, Venice was made on the second visit and shows the Ponte dell'Angelo, and the view down the Rio del Mondo Nuovo. Carolyn MacHardy has pointed out the literary associations this view held for Gagnon's contemporaries. Robert Browning's poem "Ponte dell'Angolo" (which appeared in *Asolando* on the day of his death, 12 December 1889) includes the lines,

An angel visibly guards yon house:
Above each scutcheon – a pair – stands he,
Enfolds them with droop of either wing.[3]

The selection of the composition and use of nocturnal effects in *Moonlight, Venice* were clearly influenced by Whistler's *Nocturne: Palaces* (no. 15). Unlike Whistler, Gagnon chose to depend on line rather than on plate tone to describe shadow, echoing more closely the technique of Walter Sickert (no. 61). He only used plate tone to create effects of translucency on the surface of the water.

Gagnon was a friend of the American artist Donald Shaw MacLaughlan (1876-1938) (no. 51), and it is likely that he pulled proofs of this etching on MacLaughlan's press in Paris in 1906. His use of warm black ink and golden Japanese paper demonstrates his concern with Whistlerian refinement and the *belle épreuve*.

Although he only made thirty-four copper plates, Gagnon has been credited with stimulating interest in etching in Canada early in this century, an interest manifested in the first major print exhibition in this country, the *Black and White* loan exhibition mounted by the new Art Museum of Toronto (now the Art Gallery of Ontario) in April-May 1912. Gagnon stopped etching after his return to Canada because he felt that this country was not sufficiently picturesque. He also felt that colour was essential to the depiction of life in French Canada, to which he devoted much of his career.

1 I have largely depended in this entry on the material compiled on the subject by Carolyn MacHardy in her article "Clarence Gagnon's European Etchings, 1905-1905", *RACAR* 11 (1984): 117-123.

2 "Les Salons de 1906", *Gazette des Beaux-Arts* 36 (*juillet* 1906): 60-61. Quoted in MacHardy, "Clarence Gagnon": 120.

3 MacHardy, "Clarence Gagnon": 119-120.

45   Francis Seymour Haden
British (1818-1910)
Battersea Reach 1863
Sch. 48 IV/IV
Etching and drypoint in black ink on laid paper
15 x 22.6 cm
Gift from the Canadian Imperial Bank of
Commerce Fund, 1977
Acc. no. 77/32

Francis Seymour Haden was Whistler's brother-in-law. A surgeon by profession, he had learnt to etch while studying medicine in Paris. He began to collect etchings after setting up his London practice in 1845, concentrating on

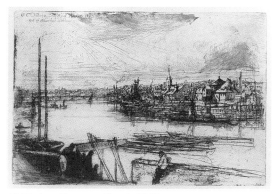

45 Haden, *Battersea Reach*, 1863

Rembrandt and the seventeenth-century Dutch school.

Whistler lived with his half-sister Deborah and her husband, at their comfortable home at 62 Sloane Street in South Kensington, when he was fourteen, in 1848-49. Haden's enthusiasm for etching, especially the etchings of Rembrandt, was an important influence on the developing artist.

In January, 1858, while recuperating from an illness, Whistler appears to have stayed with the Hadens for almost three months. It was during this sojourn that he made his first significant etchings, using the Haden children as models. Haden was stimulated into etching from life by Whistler's success, an event that marks the beginning of his lifelong career as an etcher. For some years the two men indulged their enthusiasm for etching whenever they were together, and frequently worked side-by-side from the same subject. They began to work on Thames subjects during the summer of 1859, Whistler selecting the dock area around Rotherhithe and Wapping, and Haden the bucolic reaches of the river, to which he repaired with his fishing rod and his copper plates on fine days.

After moving to London, Whistler settled along the Chelsea waterfront. In March 1863, he moved into a house at 7 Lindsay Row (now Cheyne Walk) with a studio overlooking the river. On a visit to the house Haden made this etching, which was annotated in its early states, "out of Whistler's window." It shows the influence of Whistler's Thames etchings of 1859: with its strong dark line, high horizon, and foreground *repoussoir* figure, it can be compared with *Black Lion Wharf* (no. 5). The interest in weather and atmospheric effect, which Haden explores rather clumsily in this plate, is anticipated in Whistler's etchings of 1861-63.

This impression was published in the *Gazette des Beaux-Arts* in 1864.

46 *The Towing Path* 1864
Sch. 72 VI/XVI
Drypoint in black ink on laid paper
13.8 x 21.4 cm (imp.)
Signed in pencil below plate right "Seymour Haden"
Gift of Dora Mavor Moore, on behalf of the
Mavor family, in memory of her father,
Professor James Mavor, 1976.
Acc. no. 76/67

Haden's early Thames drypoints are among the finest prints ever made in England; of them, he considered this to be one of his best.

The Towing Path, made near Hampton Court, demonstrates the sureness of his touch, and the rich, painterly effects he obtained with his needle after long hours spent poring over his Rembrandt landscape drypoints. The figure, probably that of his daughter, recalls Whistler's drypoint portrait, *Annie Haden* (K. 62), dated 1860. At this time the styles of the two men were so close as to be almost indistinguishable: the lack of "finish" in the landscape, the high horizon line, and the foreshortened picture space recall Whistler's Thames etchings of 1859.

While there was always a certain amount of friction between the two men, their devotion to Deborah and to etching enabled them to overcome their baser instincts for some years. They began to plan a joint publication of their Thames etchings, to be entitled "The Thames from its Source to the Sea", in 1863. Whistler would have contributed plates of the river as it passed through London, while Haden would have contributed studies, such as this, of its more rural reaches.

Early in 1864, a series of quarrels of growing intensity took place, and the project was finally abandoned. Whistler was very jealous of the praise heaped on Haden's Thames etchings by Philippe Burty, the Paris critic, in the *Gazette des Beaux-Arts* in September, 1864. Burty found Haden's views of the Thames much more palatable than Whistler's.

In 1865, Burty arranged with Haden for the separate publication of his Thames etchings under the title *Études à l'eau-forte*, which contained this plate. Following their publication in 1866, the etchings were exhibited in Paris and London. The exhibition was a great success, and Haden assumed the role of apologist for the etching revival and leader of the British school of etching.

46 Haden, *The Towing Path*, 1864

47 *Old Chelsea Church* 1865
Sch. 101 IV/IV
Etching in black ink on *chine collé*
11.3 x 19.6 cm (imp.)
Gift from the Canadian Imperial Bank of Commerce
Fund, 1977
Acc. no. 76/214

In 1865, Haden made the etching *Old Chelsea Church*, which shows (in reverse) Whistler's house in the centre, Old Battersea Bridge to the left, and the church tower in the distance (fig. 3). The right-hand side of the plate originally included a frontal view of a boat on whose deck a black man sat looking at the viewer. A few cables may still be seen in the lower right corner. Only one impression was pulled from the plate in this state. The composition was closely modelled on the formula Whistler had devised in his early Thames etchings. Whistler would have been outraged had he seen the first state, as he would have felt that Haden had stolen both his subject and style. This was not to be: for whatever reason, the boat and figure were removed at the request of the Secretary of the Etching Club prior to its publication in *Etchings for the Art Union of London* in 1872.

In April 1867, Whistler and his brother William (see no. 37) had an argument with Haden in a Paris restaurant following the death of Haden's medical partner, James Reeves Traer. In the scuffle that ensued, Whistler pushed Haden

through a plate glass window. Their relationship ended on the spot.[1] Although the Traer incident was the immediate cause, Whistler's professional jealousy of Haden's success as an etcher was the underlying issue.

1 For a full discussion of the incident, see Katharine Lochnan, *The Etchings of James McNeill Whistler*, pp. 145-46.

48 Charles Keene
British (1823-1891)
Edwin Edwards Reading
Ch. 6
Etching and drypoint in black ink with
plate tone on laid paper
11.3 x 10.1 cm (imp.)
Purchase, 1983
Acc. no. 83/36

Keene was an excessively modest man, best known for his wood-engraved illustrations for *Punch*, and maintained that he had only taken up etching " 'to compel myself to be certain in my line.' "[1] He was a founding member of the Junior Etching Club, and it was in this context that Whistler first met him in 1860. In 1862, inspired by Keene, Whistler made a small number of wood-engraved illustrations.[2]

Whistler considered Keene "the greatest English artist since Hogarth," and his admiration continued to the end

47 Haden, *Old Chelsea Church*, 1865

48 Keene, *Edwin Edwards Reading*

of his life.[3] Keene agreed to testify for Whistler at the Ruskin trial, although he was never called, and Whistler proposed Keene as an honourary member of the Society of British Artists in 1887. Following Keene's death in 1891, G. Somes Layard approached Whistler for information for *The Life and Letters of Charles Samuel Keene* on the strength of their mutual regard.[4]

Whistler appears to have met Edwin Edwards and his wife early in 1861 at their home at Sunbury on the Thames. Edwards was a lawyer who, when his field of jurisprudence became obselete, decided to devote himself to art and music. He was taught to etch by Whistler's friend Alphonse Legros early in 1861. Edwards became so enthusiastic that he sent to London at once for an etching press. He produced several very fine plates greatly admired by Whistler. Whistler wrote to Edwards after seeing his work at the Royal Academy in 1863, "Your etchings and your paintings I think most highly of – they are to me most *artistic*."[5]

Edwards' lovely house with its lawns stretching to the river became a meeting-place for French and English *avant garde* artists and etchers, including Whistler, Fantin-Latour, Bracquemond, Bonvin, Manet and Keene. Keene probably met Edwards on 28 February 1863, when the latter noted in his diary "C. Keene seems full of pleasant fun and humour. Tells a story well."[6] By 1864, Keene was on close terms with the Edwards, and a frequent guest at their home. Ruth Edwards, who had learnt to print by watching Auguste Delâtre, printed Charles Keene's etchings, and he maintained that there was "hardly a better printer than this lady to be found in London."[7]

This study of Edwards sitting on the lawn was probably made about this time. Keene was "profoundly impressed" by Whistler's drypoint portraits of 1859 and 1860, such as

Drouet (no. 9), in which the essential details were incised with long hair-like lines, and inessentials omitted or barely suggested. Keene would not use drypoint, considering it a weakness; however, this naturalistic study of Edwards captures the looseness of Whistler's drypoint line, and eliminates all but essential detail.

The Edwardses finally lost patience with Whistler after the Traer affair, and Ruth Edwards told the Pennells that "his conceit was his ruin – he might have been the greatest artist of his age, he simply lost his head." They never quarrelled, but simply lost contact with each other.[8]

1 Derek Hudson, *Charles Keene* (London: Pleiades Books, 1947), p. 22; quoted by Robert H. Getscher in *The Stamp of Whistler* (Oberlin, Ohio: Allen Memorial Art Museum, 1977), p. 107.

2 Daphne Du Maurier, *The Young George du Maurier: A Selection of his Letters, 1860-7* (London, 1951), p. 4. Whistler's wood-engraved illustrations may be seen in the Garrow Collection in the E.P. Taylor Reference Library of the Art Gallery of Ontario.

3 Pennell, *Life*, vol. 2, p. 231.

4 George Somes Layard to Whistler, 28 July 1891, GUL BP 11 L/4.

5 Whistler to Edwards, 1 May 1863, GUL BP II Res d/3.

6 George Somes Layard, *The Life and Letters of Charles Keene*, (London, 1892), p. 173.

7 Layard, *Life*, p. 38.

8 Ruth Edwards to Joseph Pennell, n.d., LC PC.

49 *Mrs. Edwards in a Sunbonnet*
Ch. 8
Etching printed in black ink with plate tone on laid paper
11.3 x 10.2 cm (imp.)
Purchase, 1983
Acc. no. 83/37

Keene's portrait of Ruth Edwards was executed in a completely different style from that of her husband. It is characterized by a deliberate stiffness and awkwardness of form, a naïve flattening of the picture space, and the massing of dark lines to create flat "black" areas. Such characteristics can be found in the etchings of Legros, Bracquemond, and Manet. Whistler made one plate in this manner, *Encamping* (K. 82), during a trip with Edwin Edwards in the summer of 1861. He disliked it and cancelled it after a single proof was pulled.

The dramatic figure seated in profile wearing a black dress and white sunbonnet recalls Whistler's *La Vieille aux loques* (no. 3) and anticipates both the costume and pose of his mother in *Arrangement in Grey and Black: Portrait of the Painter's Mother* (Y. 101), of 1871. There can be little doubt that Whistler and Keene exercised a mutual influence on each other at this time.

Keene requested that all his copper plates be destroyed

49 Keene, *Mrs. Edwards in a Sunbonnet*

after his death. However, Ruth Edwards, to whom he had entrusted them, left twenty-one in her attic by mistake. They were subsequently discovered, and Keene's brother authorized Goulding to print 150 sets, which were published with a preface by M.H. Spielmann in 1903. These impressions are from the Spielmann edition. Very few early impressions appear to have been taken from the plates.

50   Donald Shaw MacLaughlan
American (1876-1938)
Rushing Tide 1913
Black ink and plate tone on antique wove paper
24.7 x 29.5 cm (imp.)
Signed in pencil below plate right
Gift of Touche Ross, 1979
Acc. no. 79/123

Donald Shaw MacLaughlan was born in Charlottetown, Prince Edward Island, of Scottish descent. His family left Canada for Boston in 1890, when he was fourteen years of age. He later became a naturalized American citizen.[1] After studying at the Boston Normal Art School, he went to Paris in 1898 to study at the Atelier Gérôme. Two of his etchings were accepted by the Salon de la Société Nationale des Beaux-Arts in 1903, and the following year he was made an Associate.

MacLaughlan was influenced by Rembrandt and Whistler. He studied Rembrandt's etchings in the Cabinet des Estampes at the Bibliothèque Nationale, and was entrusted by the French government to reprint a number of Rembrandt's plates. He was a friend of the Canadian etcher, Clarence Gagnon (no. 44), who may have helped him exe-

cute this commission.[2]

MacLaughlan followed in Whistler's footsteps, working in London, Paris and Venice, creating plates that owe a clear debt to Whistler. Whether or not he ever met Whistler face-to-face, he certainly claimed a unique relationship to him in that he believed that he had three times been contacted by Whistler in séances! This is not inappropriate, as Whistler himself had attended numerous séances during the period of his friendship with the Pre-Raphaelite artist Dante Gabriel Rossetti. The first two occasions were recorded by the Pennells in their entry in *The Whistler Journal* for 13 March 1910.[3] On the first occasion, a mysterious spirit ultimately identified as that of a French artist claimed to have a message for MacLaughlan from Whistler. The message was that "Whistler wished MacLaughlan to go on with his etching, to devote himself to it." Later, in Florence, soon after the MacLaughlans had been reading the Pennells' *Life of Whistler*, Whistler's own spirit is said to have told MacLaughlan that he must go on with his etching.

On the strength of MacLaughlan's experiences, a special séance was organized by a Mrs. Sauter on 31 March 1910, which the Pennells attended. They described the event as follows:

The séance was held in the studio, round a large mahogany table on casters, lights out and silence. There was nothing for some time. Then the table trembled, moved about, raised itself on two legs, pushed us out of our chairs. At last it rapped, but in answer to no letter of the alphabet except W., when, however, excepting once or twice, it rapped vigorously. Occasionally it rapped yes or no to a question: No, it did not want to give a message to anybody. No, it did not want music. Yes, it did want something. What? A drink. MacLaughlan said an impish power was about, but a strong one. It was asked whether its name was William, Wilfred or Winifred, Sauter asked it in German whether it spoke Italian and Mrs. Sauter in Italian whether it spoke German, but no answer. The fire began to go out. The studio got cold. Sauter, Joseph, Withers and Dulac went downstairs. After that, no more "manifestations" except trembling and vibration, and at last

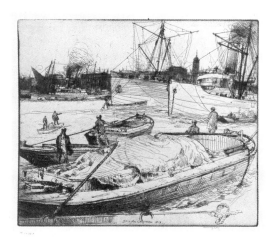

50 MacLaughlan, *Rushing Tide*, 1913

everybody decided to go down and "get a drink" with the spirit. As we were going, Mrs. Sauter suddenly regretted that nobody had thought of asking it if it was Whistler. And then we got down stairs to be told by J. that after the first tremblings and pushings, which he fancied came from one or another of the party, he decided to see whether this was so, or whether a power stronger than he was at work, and the rest of the manifestations came from his long legs! General dismay and disappointment. But for all that, experiments were tried with planchette. MacLaughlan, at a table by himself, with a clean sheet of paper before him, held a pencil in his hand making it passive for the "power" to write with. A message came: "Whistler is among you this evening. He wants your friends to try again." Of course we all, excepting Joseph and Sauter, hurried back to see the thing through. The table could not be induced to do anything but tremble. And we went home as unbelieving as we came.[4]

Whatever the truth of the matter, it is clear that MacLaughlan saw his own work as being closely tied to that of Whistler. He followed Whistler's precepts, grinding his own ink, seeking out fine old papers, and printing all his plates himself. In this view of the Thames, his clear dark line resembles that found in Whistler's Thames etchings of 1859. MacLaughlan used Whistler's device of leading the eye into the composition by placing a large boat on an angle in the foreground, and focused the attention of the viewer in the lower left corner of the plate. Although his work owes a great debt to Whistler, MacLaughlan handled his large plates vigorously, and never lost his own artistic identity, unlike many of the posthumous followers.

1 Biographical questionnaire, National Academy of Design, New York. This information was published by Carolyn MacHardy in "Clarence Gagnon": 121, note 27.

2 MacHardy, "Clarence Gagnon": 121.

3 Pennell, *Whistler Journal*, p. 159.

4 Pennell, *Whistler Journal*, pp. 160-61.

51 James McBey
Scottish (1883-1959)
The Deserted Palace 1925
C. 236
Etching in brown ink on old grey laid paper
21 x 25.3 cm (imp.)
Signed in ink lower right "James McBey" and numbered "III"
Edition: 80 proofs
Gift of Touche Ross, 1979
Acc. no. 79/126

James McBey was born in Newmill, near Aberdeen, Scotland. His father, whom he saw only once, was a farmer; he and his mother lived with his grandmother, to whom he was devoted. His depressive mother showed him no affection and committed suicide when he was still a young man.

McBey taught himself to etch from Maxime Lalanne's *Treatise on Etching*, which he found in a library in 1902. It is hardly surprising, since his development took place in the years following Whistler's death and the memorial exhibitions, that McBey was profoundly influenced by him. Nowhere does he demonstrate his debt to Whistler more clearly than in his Venice etchings.

McBey visited Venice in the autumn of 1924 and 1925. The etchings which were made on these visits were issued in three sets: eight in 1926, seven in 1928, and nine in 1930. They were regarded as the summit of McBey's career, and were so highly thought of that Colnaghi's, the London print dealership, paid £5,250 for the trial proofs of the first eight plates, pulled in 1928.[1] McBey, more than any artist of the period, was able to ride the wave of popularity unleashed by Whistler, which carried the prices of etchings to dizzy heights until the collapse of the stock market in 1929. He printed all his own plates in editions that never exceeded eighty proofs, and there was always a long list of people waiting for impressions.

In none of the plates does McBey come closer to Whistler than in *The Deserted Palace*, which he made on 16 Octo-

51 McBey, *The Deserted Palace*, 1925

ber 1925. Here he employed a characteristic Whistler subject, a frontal image of a doorway reflected in a canal, with a gondola leading the eye to the centre of the composition. It can be compared to Whistler's Venice etching *Two Doorways* (K. 193), of l879. McBey exercised more restraint than usual in this plate; he avoided his tendency toward heavy, "fuzzy" lines, in favour of small clusters of short, hairlike lines in the manner of Whistler.

McBey's work is, for the most part, passionate, energetic and romantic in a way that recalls J.M.W. Turner as much as Whistler. In a sea of uninspired followers, he managed to make of the Whistler inheritance something distinctly his own – which is refreshing, when one looks at the hundreds of imitative Venice etchings churned out by his generation.

1 James McBey, *The Early Life of James McBey: An Autobiography 1883-1911*, ed. by Nicolas Barker (Oxford: Oxford University Press, 1977), p. 124.

52   John Marin
American (1870-1953)
Piazzetta, San Marco 1907
Z. 65
Etching and drypoint in black ink with plate tone on Japanese paper
17 x 22.9 cm
Signed in pencil lower right "John Marin"
Edition: about 30 proofs
Gift from the Collection of Anna Hoyt Mavor, Director Emeritus of the Print and Drawing Department, Boston Museum of Fine Arts, 1979.
Acc. no. 79/8

Marin was raised in Weehawken, New Jersey, across the Hudson River from Manhattan. After working for a number of architects in the 1890s, he set up his own office. In 1899 he entered the Pennsylvania Academy of the Fine Arts in Philadelphia where William Merritt Chase, a friend of Whistler's, was teaching at the time.[1] The students at the Academy were apparently divided into John Singer Sargent and Whistler camps: Marin became a Whistler sympathiser.

He went to Paris in September 1905, where his step-brother, Charles Bittinger, found him a studio and provided him with etching equipment. He taught himself technique from Maxime Lalanne's handbook on etching, and hoped to supplement a small income from his father by the sale of his etchings. He travelled to Amsterdam, Venice and London making etchings.

In 1907, the year in which his work was accepted in the Salon d'Automne, he went to Venice and stayed with his father, stepmother and the Bittingers at the Pension Gregory. Marin refused to visit the exhibition of Whistler's Venetian etchings that was on at the Accademia at the time, being afraid that it might influence him. Nonetheless, as Carl Zigrosser has pointed out, Whistler's prestige was at its peak at this time, and "no young etcher could escape its pervasive authority."[2]

Whistler's influence can be clearly seen in *Piazzetta San Marco*, which is closely related in subject, composition and style to Whistler's *The Piazzetta* (K. 189), dated 1879-80. Like Whistler, Marin worked directly from the subject without reversing the plate. He chose a view of San Marco seen from the Ducal Palace, while Whistler had selected a view looking past San Marco toward the clock tower. Marin, following Whistler's example, included a vertical element, a column in place of the campanile, which divides the space into asymmetrical compartments and is truncated in the upper reaches of the composition. Marin also imitated Whistler's style very closely in this plate, using his line selectively, and printing it with a delicate film of plate tone.

Up to the time of Marin's return to America in 1911, Whistler was the chief influence on his work. As R.H. Getscher has pointed out, Marin seems to echo Whistler in the explanation of his method published in 1909: "One might call an etching a written impression of tone, more or less in the spirit of a veil to soften, as does nature's veil soften, her harshness of line."[3]

In 1910, Alfred Steiglitz gave Marin his first one-man show at the Photo-Secession Gallery in New York. After his return to America the following year, he was influenced by the Cézannes, Picassos and Matisses he saw at Steiglitz's gallery, and produced a dynamic series of abstract studies of New York. Marin became a pioneer of American abstract painting, and participated in the Armory Show of 1913.

1 Allen Staley, ed., *From Realism to Symbolism: Whistler and his World* (New York: Columbia University, 1971), pp. 66-67.

2 Carl Zigrosser, *The Complete Etchings of John Marin* (Philadelphia: Philadelphia Museum of Art, 1969), p. 11.

3 Quoted in Getscher, *The Stamp of Whistler*, p. 254.

53   Mortimer Menpes
Australian (1855-1938)
Limehouse
Etching in black ink on laid paper
23.1 x 27.3 cm (imp.)
Gift from the Canadian Imperial Bank of Commerce Fund, 1977
Acc. no. 76/211

Menpes was born in Australia and probably came to England when his family returned there in 1875. He studied at the South Kensington Schools under Edward J. Poynter, who was a friend of Whistler during student days in Paris.

Menpes first encountered Whistler in November 1880, a few days after his return from Venice, when his fortunes were at their lowest ebb. They met in the little room over the Fine Art Society in Bond Street that had been set up to provide Whistler with a place to print the "First Venice Set", which was due to go on display at the end of the month.

Menpes offered to help with the printing, abandoning his studies to became Whistler's first "follower." One day when Whistler was having difficulties at the press, he asked Menpes to print one of his "Palaces" (probably no. 15). The result was so good that Menpes printed regularly for Whistler from then on.

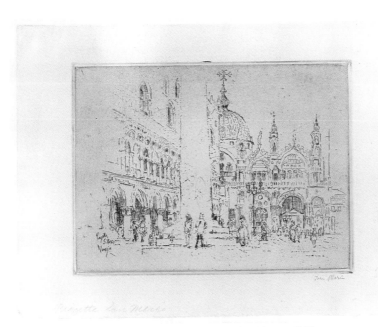

52 Marin, *Piazzetta, San Marco*, 1907

53 Menpes, *Limehouse*

Whistler chose to view his "follower" as an extension of himself, just as the Japanese printmaker viewed his apprentices. He said to him, "I have educated and trained you, and have created an atmosphere which enables you to carry out my intentions exactly as I myself should. You are but the medium translating the ideas of the master."[1] Menpes, assisted at times by his wife, Dorothy, continued to print for Whistler for several years.

Menpes maintained that Whistler taught him to etch, and during the early 1880s he was able to observe Whistler closely. His mastery of Whistler's methods, and his role as "follower," led him to imitate the "Master" quite successfully. In this view of the docks near Rotherhithe, Menpes employed the subject-matter and the clean dark line Whistler had used in his Thames etchings of 1859 (no. 5), combined with elements from the Venice etchings. He eliminated the device of the foreground *repoussoir* figure in favour of a "floating" view, which can be compared with *Nocturne* (no. 13). Menpes' subtle use of plate tone to create atmospheric effect shows the result of Whistler's tutelage in the printing of the Venice etchings.

Because Whistler needed Menpes to print for him, he overlooked some of the things that annoyed him. Menpes was much too friendly with Haden, and joined the Society of Painter-Etchers in 1881. Whistler tried to overlook these infractions, and went on trips with Menpes to St. Ives in 1884 and to Holland in 1885. In 1886, Whistler's tone became frosty; the following year, Menpes committed the unpardonable crime of going to Japan, a journey Whistler felt should have been left first to the "Master." When Menpes exhibited his Japanese works, he refused to sign himself "pupil of Whistler." This was followed by other examples of insubordination, which tried Whistler's patience until finally, in 1889, he instructed the "kangaroo" to "go to Spain and blow his brains out."[2]

Menpes managed to forget his bitterness after Whistler's death in 1903, and within a month was concerned to raise a monument to him.[3] However, in November he sold his collection of Whistler etchings at the Leicester Galleries. In 1904 he published an excellent book of reminiscences, *Whistler as I Knew Him*, in which he described Whistler's methods of inking, biting and printing in great detail.

1 Mortimer Menpes, *Whistler as I Knew Him* (London: Adam and Charles Black, 1904), p. 100.

2 Whistler to Menpes, 28 March 1889, GUL BP 111 G/69.

3 William Heinemann to Rosalind Birnie Philip, 4 August 1903, GUL BP H. 202.

54 Joseph Pennell
American (1860-1926)
Whitehall Court from Westminster 1903
W. 275
Etching in black ink with plate tone
on *papier bleuté*
26.5 x 20 cm (imp.)
Signed in pencil below centre "J. Pennell imp."
Edition: 60 impressions
Gift of Sir Edmund Walker Estate, 1926
Acc. no. 1547

Joseph Pennell is best known as Whistler's biographer, but was in his own right a printmaker of considerable ability. He was born into a Philadelphia Quaker family, and despite the Friends' opposition, was supported in his ambition to become an artist by his father. Having applied unsuccessfully for entry into the Pennsylvania Academy of the Fine Arts in the fall of 1876, he finally gained admission in 1879. In 1880, he left the Academy and received his first commissions for illustrations from *Scribner's Monthly* and *The Century* magazines.

Pennell learned to etch from Stephen Ferris who helped to found the New York Etching Club in 1877 and the Philadelphia Society of Etchers in 1880. Through Ferris, Pennell became a founding member and Secretary to the Philadelphia Society. Meetings were sometimes held at the

54 Pennell, *Whitehall Court from Westminster*, 1903

home of James L. Claghorn, President of the Pennsylvania Academy, and it was in Claghorn's collection that Pennell first saw the etchings of Whistler. Pennell saw Whistler's "First Venice Set," which Ernest G. Brown of the Fine Art Society brought over from London, in 1881. In 1882, the Academy held an exhibition in which works by Whistler were shown.

Pennell first went to Europe in 1883 on a commission from *The Century* magazine, and hoped to meet Whistler at this time. He carried a letter of introduction to Whistler's brother, Dr. William Whistler (see no. 37), but it was not until July 1884, that Pennell was able to call on Whistler in Chelsea. He invited Whistler to make some illustrations of Old Chelsea for *The Century*; Whistler declined, but immediately volunteered the services of Mortimer Menpes, who was in the same room (no. 53). Pennell quickly said that he would do the illustrations himself.

Pennell did not really become an intimate until the spring of 1893 when he and his wife, the writer Elizabeth Robins, were often at the Whistlers' home on the rue du Bac in Paris. Whistler asked Pennell to help bite and print his Paris etchings in 1893. Working with Whistler rekindled Pennell's interest in etching.

It was at the time of Mrs. Whistler's illness and after her death that the Pennells attached themselves firmly to Whistler. They began to collect information for a biography in 1897, and kept fastidious notes which were used in the two-volume *Life*, published in 1908, and *The Whistler Journal*, which appeared in Philadelphia in 1921. Pennell's argumentative nature and blind adulation was put to good use by Whistler, who was concerned to ensure his own immortality. Despite the fact that the Pennells must have annoyed Whistler, they provided assistance, hospitality and much-needed companionship after the death of Beatrice, and there was never a falling out. Edward Kennedy appears to have expected something of the kind when he wrote to Whistler, "I notice that there is some fighting again in the Latin Quarter, so that the riotous Quaker Pennell will have a chance to get shot or stabbed or something yet."[1]

The Pennells lived in a flat on Buckingham Street in an apartment overlooking the Thames. Although it was small, Elizabeth Robins wrote that "the curtains were never drawn on the one spectacle we could offer – the river with the boats trailing their lights down its shadowy reaches."[2] Like Whistler, Joseph Pennell was drawn to the river. *Whitehall Court from Westminster* was made in the year of Whistler's death, and clearly owes a debt to his Venice nocturnes, and to his lithotint, *Nocturne: The River at Battersea* (no. 23).

An orthodox follower, Pennell had his etching tools fashioned, like Whistler, by a dentist, and washed acid about on the surface of the plate to bite it. He printed his own plates, leaving, in this instance, a film of plate tone on the surface to achieve the desired nocturnal effect. Having accompanied Whistler on many paper chases, he developed an insatiable appetite for fine old papers; this impression is printed on a choice piece of *papier bleuté*.

1 Edward Kennedy to Whistler, n.d., GUL BP 11 37/50.

2 Elizabeth Pennell, *Nights*, p. 212.

55   *Building the Building*
no. 8 in the *Iconophiles Set* 1904
W. 160
Transfer lithograph on old laid paper
32.6 x 23.1 cm (sheet)
Gift of Mr. and Mrs. Ralph Presgrave, 1978
Acc. no. 78/64

At the time Pennell became a Whistler intimate, Whistler's interest in etching was being eclipsed by his preoccupation with lithography. It is therefore not surprising that Pennell took up transfer lithography in the manner of Whistler. In October 1893, Pennell attended a lecture-demonstration of lithography which Whistler's printer Thomas Way gave at the Art Worker's Guild in London, and tried some of the transfer paper handed out to the audience.

In 1895, Pennell wrote the introduction to a catalogue of Whistler lithographs exhibited at the Fine Art Society, and, in turn, Whistler wrote the introduction to the catalogue of Pennell's lithographs shown at the Fine Art Society in 1896. Pennell observed Whistler at work on his lithographic portrait of *Mallarmé* (W. 66), dated 1894, and both Joseph and Elizabeth Robins sat for Whistler lithographs four times in 1896 (no. 38).[1]

Walter Sickert attacked Pennell for his use of transfer lithography in the *Saturday Review* in 1897, writing that "to pass off drawings made on paper as lithographs was as misleading to the purchaser on the vital point of commer-

55 Pennell, *Building the Building*, 1904

cial value, as to sell photogravures for etchings." Pennell sued for libel. Whistler appeared as a witness for Pennell, and declared that there was no limit to what could be done by the transfer process, and that the artist working on paper was at no disadvantage to the artist working on stone. Pennell won the case.

Pennell was concerned to learn the secret of transferring the drawing from transfer paper to stone, which the Ways refused ever to divulge. He learnt the process from Charles Goulding, the brother of Frederick Goulding, the printer of etchings. It was Charles Goulding who printed the posthumous editions of Whistler's lithographs for Miss Birnie Philip.[2]

The year after Whistler's death, in 1904, Joseph Pennell visited New York, and was very struck by the skyscrapers that were going up everywhere. They immediately became his favorite New York subject, either built, or in the more picturesque stage of being built. Pennell came to the conclusion that work was the greatest thing in the modern world, and would later coin the phrase "the wonder of work" to describe one of his major themes. His interest in modern life can be seen as a logical sequence to Whistler's early realist orientation.

Building the Building was inspired by the construction of Wanamakers in Philadelphia. In the omission of all but a few architectural details, and in the drawing of shadows rather than contours, as well as in the shorthand style used for the figures, this work is close to Whistler's lithographs and can be compared with the *Victoria Club* (W. 11), of 1879. It is more labored and "finished" than comparable prints by Whistler, but Pennell comes as close as William Rothenstein (fig. 8, no. 58) to capturing the essentials of Whistler's style in the unusual technique of transfer lithography. The title makes it clear that Pennell was interested in the design of the building under construction, not in the building itself.

1 *Firelight*, W. 103, *Firelight: Joseph Pennell*, W. 104, *Firelight: Joseph Pennell No.2.*, W. 105, and *The Russian Schube*, W. 112.

2 Louis A. Wuerth, *Catalogue of the Lithographs of Joseph Pennell* (Boston, Mass.: Little, Brown and Co., 1931), p. xiii.

56 Matthew White Ridley
British (1837-1888)
Durham
Etching on *chine collé*
13.5 x 21.3 cm (imp.)
Gift from the Canadian Imperial Bank of Commerce Fund, 1978
Acc. no. 77/159

Ridley was born in Newcastle, England.[1] In 1856, despite his father's wishes that he become an architect, he became a probationer at the Royal Academy Schools. He was not admitted as a full student until 1858, and it was probably during the intervening years that he went to Paris to study painting at the Académie Julian.

Ridley met Whistler in Paris in 1856-57, while the latter was at Gleyre's Academy, and became part of the "English

56 Ridley, *Durham*

Group," which included Whistler, E.J. Poynter, George du Maurier and Thomas Armstrong (fig. 2). A few years later he met Edwin Edwards (see no. 48) in a drawing class in London, and introduced Legros, Whistler and Fantin to him. This led to the formation of the so-called "Suffolk," or Anglo-French, school of etchers, which looked upon Sunbury, on the River Thames, as home.

Whistler probably taught Ridley to etch, and seems to have looked upon him as a pupil. Such views of shipping as *Durham* were influenced by Whistler's Thames etchings of 1859 and 1860. Ridley adopted the deliberate *naïveté* that characterized the work of Alphonse Legros and Edwards, and which made a brief appearance in Whistler's work at this time. The contrast between the very detailed handling of the boats and the lack of detail in the sky and water are very Whistlerian.

Edwards invited Ridley and Whistler to go on an overnight camping trip with him on 18 June 1861. On this occasion Whistler made two drypoints, *Encamping* (K. 82) and *The Storm* (K. 81), in which Ridley appears. When Whistler was planning his return from Venice, he wrote to Dr. and Mrs. William Whistler asking them to tell Ridley to keep the printing press in good order, "for when I come back I shall retire to his studio and print all my proofs."[2] This did not in fact happen.

1 Valerie Gatty, "Artists' Fruitful Friendship", *Country Life* 7 March 1974: 507-508.

2 Whistler to Dr. and Mrs. William Whistler (from Venice), (1880), LC PC.

57 Auguste Rodin
French (1840-1917)
Victor Hugo, De Trois Quarts 1864
L.D. 6 VI/VIII
Drypoint printed with plate tone on wove paper
22.3 x 15.1 cm (imp.)
Gift of Mr. and Mrs. Ralph Presgrave, 1976
Acc. no. 76/244

Rodin and Whistler were both students in Paris during the 1850s. Like Whistler's friends Fantin-Latour and Legros, Rodin studied under Lecoq de Boisbaudran.

VICTOR HUGO

57 Rodin, *Victor Hugo, De Trois Quarts*, 1864

Rodin requires no introduction as the greatest sculptor of his generation; his prints are less well known. His first drypoint was made on the back of one of Alphonse Legros' copper plates at the latter's home in London in 1861, and it appears likely that Legros taught him the drypoint technique.

The portrait of Victor Hugo, made three years later, is closer to Whistler's drypoint portraits of 1859 than it is to the drypoints of Legros. It recalls Whistler's powerful portrait of *Drouet* (no. 9), with its loose, bravura line and concentration on facial detail, while giving the body only cursory treatment.

Whistler may have been influenced by Rodin's drawings and watercolours of thinly draped nude figures when he returned to this theme in lithography in 1890. In addition, his lithograph of Joseph Pennell wearing an enormous cape, entitled *The Russian Schube* (W. 112), recalls Rodin's bulbous portrait of Balzac of 1892-98, which Whistler told Pennell he disliked.[1] Rodin visited Whistler in Paris and London in the 1890s, and the two admired each other's work. Following Whistler's death, Rodin wrote an appreciation of Whistler to the Pennells in which he commented on how well Whistler drew, and added "*L'oeuvre de Whistler ne perdra jamais par le temps; elle gagnera; car une de ses forces est l'énergie, une autre la délicatesse; mais la principale est l'étude de dessin.*"[2]

Rodin succeeded Whistler as President of the Interna-tional Society of Sculptors, Painters and Gravers. He was invited by the Society to design a memorial to his predecessor. Instead of the winged victory symbolizing Whistler's triumph, "The Triumph of Art over the Enemies," which had been agreed upon, Rodin designed a realist "Venus" climbing the mountain of "Fame." In doing so, Rodin was undoubtedly thinking more of Whistler's sharp tongue and mannerisms than of his aesthetic goals. The monument was never completed; Rodin died in 1917, and the International Society rejected the design.

1 Pennell, *Whistler Journal*, p. 201.

2 Pennell, *Life*, vol. 2, p. 278.

58   William Rothenstein
British (1872-1942)
Portrait of Sir Francis Seymour Haden 1897
Transfer lithograph on laid paper
38 x 25.2 cm (sheet)
Gift of Touche Ross, 1979
Acc. no. 79/127

William Rothenstein was a student of Alphonse Legros at the Slade School in 1888. After seeing his first Whistler paintings hanging at a girl's school, he returned to the Slade "full of excitement", only to discover that "Legros strongly disapproved of Whistler's influence."[1] Whistler and Legros had fallen out in 1867, and had not spoken since.

Rothenstein first met Whistler in Paris, after enrolling in the Académie Julian. He greatly admired the quality of Whistler's draughtsmanship, and felt very shy upon being introduced at the home of Miss Ruebell in 1892.[2] He recalled how "To me Whistler was almost a legendary figure, whom I never thought to meet in the flesh." He found Beatrice Whistler "an ample and radiant figure" who was amused and pleased by the reverence that Rothenstein felt for her husband.[3] During the week that followed, Whistler turned up unannounced at Rothenstein's studio to see his work. The following day a note arrived inviting him to dine at the apartment on the rue du Bac into which the Whistlers had recently moved.

Whistler charmed young Rothenstein, whose memoirs have left us with a vivid and sympathetic portrait of the artist in his last decade. With Whistler, according to Rothenstein, "One walked delicately, but in an enchanted garden."[4] He was bitter about England, but endlessly interested in his visitors, always wanting to know what they were doing and whom they were seeing. On Sunday at the rue du Bac, "while talking to his visitors he usually had a little copper plate in his hands, on which he would scratch from time to time."[5]

Rothenstein met Whistler just as he was dropping etching in favour of lithography.[6] When Rothenstein was commissioned to make a series of portraits to be published as *Oxford Characters*, Whistler encouraged him to use lithography and put him in touch with the Ways in London. T.R. Way wrote to Whistler on 3 November 1893, "Mr. Rothenstein is making some charming portraits on the paper, he

58 Rothenstein,
Portrait of Sir Francis Seymour Haden, 1897

on transfer paper, was executed in a style modelled closely on Whistler's. It might even be viewed as a pendant to Whistler's portrait, entitled *Unfinished Sketch of Lady Haden* (Way 143), of 1895. A sensitive study, it captures the appearance of a man whose vision is failing, and who appears to be feeling his way across the copper.

Whistler, who had originally promised to sit for one of the portraits, later declined Rothenstein's request, saying that "two Napoleons at a time" were surely enough in any series, one of them being "the apothecary of Hants."[11] Haden was very upset that he was not shown his portrait or the biography that accompanied it, prior to their publication.[12] Rothenstein, unable to please either side, suffered the usual fate of those who found themselves caught between Haden and Whistler.

Whistler and Rothenstein parted ways over the Sickert *vs.* Pennell court case in 1897, in which Sickert challenged the validity of transfer lithography. Rothenstein, who disliked Pennell, agreed to appear as a witness for Sickert; Whistler appeared as a witness for Pennell, who won the case. Whistler forgave this slight, but shortly thereafter saw Rothenstein in the company of his archenemy, Sir William Eden. That was the end of their friendship. After the turn of the century, Rothenstein disowned Whistler's influence.

1 William Rothenstein, *Men and Memories*, vol. 1 (London: Faber and Faber, 1931), p. 31.

2 Ibid., p. 71.

3 Ibid., p. 83.

4 Ibid., p. 84.

5 Ibid., p. 85.

6 Ibid., p. 85.

7 Way to Whistler, 3 November 1893, GUL BP 11 33/30.

8 Whistler to Way, 18 September 1894, GUL BP Res. 18e/65.

9 Rothenstein, *Men and Memories*, vol. 1, p. 306.

10 Ibid., p. 306.

11 Ibid., p. 308.

12 Ibid., p. 307.

is amazingly clever."[7] While Whistler was normally secretive about his work, he did not mind the fact that Way had shown his recent lithographs to Rothenstein, who "has written me a very nice little letter about them."[8] When Rothenstein's series appeared, Whistler subscribed to the whole set.

In 1898, Rothenstein produced *English Portraits* along much the same lines. He wrote to ask Whistler's brother-in-law Sir Francis Seymour Haden (see no. 4, and nos. 45-47) to sit for him. The elderly artist replied at once, inviting Rothenstein to Woodcote Manor, "a beautiful Tudor house, kept in marvellous order", with shining floors, polished panelling and furniture, bright brass handles and sparkling silver.[9] He found Haden "a big impressive figure whose word was law," proud of his position as President of the Painter-Etchers, and with "a marked sense of his own importance."[10] According to Rothenstein, at this time "no one, not even Whistler, had a greater European reputation as an etcher than Haden." Lady Haden, "a gracious, dignified lady, rather quiet and subdued in manner," came into the room when her husband was out, and asked rather timidly whether Rothenstein knew Whistler and whether he was a supporter or not.

Rothenstein drew Haden sitting in his workroom making a mezzotint in February 1897. The lithograph, drawn

59 Theodore Roussel
French (1847-1926)
The Street, Chelsea Embankment c. 1888
Etching and plate tone on old laid paper,
trimmed to the plate line and signed in pencil on
the tab "Theodore Roussel"
14.7 x 20.7 cm (sheet)
Gift from the Canadian Imperial Bank of Commerce
Fund, 1977
Acc. no. 76/215

Born in Lorient, Brittany, Roussel gave up a military career on account of poor health after serving in the Franco-Prussian War of 1870. He decided to become an artist, and moved to England about 1874, marrying an Englishwoman in 1879. He had been living and working in Chelsea for some years, painting its streets and shops, when his work came to Whistler's attention at Dowdeswells on Bond Street. Whistler admired Roussel's pictures, which were not unlike his own, and asked to be introduced to the artist.

Roussel greatly esteemed Whistler, and joined the small but devoted band of artists who rallied around the "Master" in his post-Venice period. Rothenstein described the group, which included Walter Sickert, Mortimer Menpes, and the Greaves brothers, as "an artistic bodyguard."[1] Menpes observed that Roussel always went bare-headed in Whistler's presence as an act of homage, in response to which Whistler said, "At last, I have found a follower worthy of the master."[2] Rothenstein, perhaps more in tune with the situation, saw Roussel as "intelligent, witty and a little *méchant*."[3]

It was at Whistler's instigation that Roussel began to etch seriously in 1887/8, soon after the publication of Whistler's *Propositions* in 1886. Roussel's early etchings demonstrate slavish adherence to the principles outlined in the *Propositions*: made on small copper plates, they were trimmed leaving a projecting tab for an autograph signature. Like Whistler, Roussel worked directly from nature, aiming for lightness and spontaneity.

Whistler was working on his London etchings at this time, and it is not surprising that Roussel's first etchings were closely modelled on Whistler's shopfronts of 1884-8. His most successful plate of the period, *The Street, Chelsea Embankment*, closely resembles Whistler's *The Fish Shop, Busy Chelsea* (K. 264), of 1887. In it, Roussel adopted the same frontal approach, using the road in the foreground to lead the eye up to the row of buildings running parallel to the picture plane. The façades are enlivened with doors, windows, and awnings, as in Whistler's etching. Roussel does not, however, achieve the poetic rhythm and abstract patterning found in Whistler. His line is somewhat coarser and bears comparison with that of Walter Sickert. Roussel, who was excessively humble, maintained that "Anything I have done in etching I owe absolutely to the influence of Whistler."[4]

1 Rothenstein, *Men and Memories*, vol. 1, p. 168.

2 Menpes, *Whistler as I Knew Him*, p. 19.

3 Rothenstein, *Men and Memories*, vol. 1, p. 18.

4 Frank Rutter, *Theodore Roussel* (London: *The Connoisseur*, 1926), p. 37.

59 Roussel, *The Street, Chelsea Embankment*, c. 1888

60 Sir Frank Short
British (1857-1945)
The Angler's Bridge on the Wandle
S. 221
Etching on laid paper
14.9 x 22.6 cm (imp.)
Signed below plate, centre
Gallery Purchase, 1930
Acc. no. 1371

Short was devoted to printmaking. After a brief career in engineering, his father's profession, he studied at the National Art Training School at South Kensington. In 1885, he was elected to the Royal Society of Painter-Etchers, where he greatly impressed Seymour Haden. He received many honours, and served as head of the Engraving School of the Royal College of Art from 1891 to 1924.

Whistler first heard from Short in 1885. Short was deeply impressed by Whistler's *The Little White Girl* and asked Whistler's permission to make an etching after the painting. He wrote that, "as a student it made such a revolution in my ideas of work that I think it ought to be known to all students of today – we do not get many chances of seeing your work."[1] Whistler enclosed a copy of the *Ten O'Clock* lecture with his reply, and Short wrote back, "many stray ideas which had been wandering about in my head of late were crystalized into form by what you said."[2]

Short quickly proved himself a master of printmaking techniques of all kinds, and Whistler went to him when he encountered technical problems in biting and printing his Paris etchings. In 1892 he wrote to Short at the Royal College of Art asking for the recipe for the "Dutch bath" and for some old paper for proofs.[3] In July 1899, Whistler, who had moved back to London, asked Frank Short for permission to use his press to print the Paris etchings. He soon accepted Short's offer to reground and print the plates.

In his etching *On the Wandle*, Short demonstrates the freshness of his *plein air* etching style, which appears to owe a debt to Whistler's etching *Sketching, No. 1* (K. 86), of 1861, published in *Passages from Modern English Poets*, and to Haden's *Egham Lock* (S. 21), dated 1859, which appeared in the *Gazette des Beaux-Arts*; both, in turn, had

been influenced by Rembrandt. It is apparent from *On the Wandle* with what ease he could synthesize the closely related Thames styles of Whistler and Haden and produce a work of his own. Short was weighted down with the nineteenth-century tradition of Whistler, Haden and Legros, and continued it loyally into the twentieth century. His most distinguished works are his reproductive mezzotints after Turner.

In his will, Seymour Haden left one hundred pounds and his gold badge of office, given by Queen Victoria to the Royal Society of Painter-Etchers, on condition that Frank Short be appointed Vice-President. He left fifty pounds to Short for having instilled in the minds of his pupils the importance of printing their own work.[4] Short served as President of the Society from 1910 to 1919.

1. Short to Whistler, 26 January 1885, GUL BP 11 s/36.

2. Short to Whistler, 22 February 1885, GUL BP LL 32/6.

3. Short to Whistler, 18 September 1892, GUL BP LL S/37.

4. Sir Francis Seymour Haden, Last Will and Testament, Public Records Office, London.

61 Walter Richard Sickert
British (1860-1942)
Maple Street c. 1920
Etching and drypoint in black ink on old laid paper
20.0 x 12.9 cm (imp.)
Purchase, 1978
Acc. no. 78/102

Sickert was born in Munich, Germany, but came to England at the age of eight. In May 1879, the month in which Whistler was declared bankrupt, he met the artist for the first time and was deeply impressed. He wrote, "Such a man! The only painter alive who has first immense genius, then conscientious persistent work striving after his ideal he knowing exactly what he is about and turned aside by no indifference or ridicule."[1]

After entering the Slade in 1881, where he was a pupil of Alphonse Legros, Sickert went to see Whistler, who encouraged him to leave, saying, " 'You've wasted your money, Walter; there's no use wasting your time too!' "[2] Sickert became a "follower" in the winter of 1881-82, and set to work with Mortimer Menpes printing Venice etchings and carting lithographic stones for the "Master." Whistler taught Sickert and Menpes his "secret of drawing," which Sickert scribbled on his shirt sleeve.

Whistler was working on his small London plates and conceiving his "Propositions" between 1880 and 1886, when they were published. It is therefore not surprising that when Sickert made his first etchings in 1883, he worked on small plates in a Whistlerian style, trimmed the margins off his proofs, and signed his name on a projecting tab. In 1883, Whistler gave him a letter of introduction to his old friend Degas, and Sickert went to Paris, where he fell under the spell of the more robust master. This was to have a decisive influence on his etching style.

60 Short, *The Angler's Bridge on the Wandle*

fig. 10, Sickert. *Study for 'O Sole Mio.'* Pencil, pen and black ink, squared off in red ink, 19.8 x 12.6 cm, Art Gallery of Ontario, Purchase, 1978.

MAPLE STREET

61 Sickert, *Maple Street*, c. 1920

Sickert remained on good terms with Whistler for a long time, despite his growing independence. In 1893 he opened the Chelsea Life School in The Vale, with Whistler as patron; William Rothenstein (fig. 8, no. 58) was among those who attended his night classes. In 1884 Sickert went to St. Ives with Whistler and Menpes, and Whistler stayed with Sickert in Dieppe in 1885. Sickert organized a large exhibition of Whistler's work at the Working Man's College in Bloomsbury in 1889.

Whistler and Sickert fell out over the Eden affair, which preoccupied Whistler following the tragic death of his wife in 1896, and gave rise to Whistler's pamphlet *The Baronet and the Butterfly*. The relationship ended in 1897 after Sickert attacked the validity of transfer lithography in an article in *The Saturday Review*. Pennell sued for libel, and won the case with the help of Whistler, who appeared as a witness. After this, Whistler dismissed Sickert as "an insignificant and irresponsible person."[3]

Although the effects of Whistler's influence were greatly altered by Sickert's encounter with Degas, they still linger in his street scenes and low-life subjects. *Maple Street*, which was not made until c. 1920, owes a debt to Whistler's early etching *Street at Saverne* (no. 2), his Chelsea nocturne paintings of the 1870s, and his London street scenes of the 1880s. The patterning and verticality of the composition recall the Amsterdam etchings of 1889.

Sickert took issue with many of Whistler's maxims concerning etching. He often made preparatory drawings, as he did for this one (fig. 10), rejecting Whistler's concept of working directly from nature. His much more robust line, with its ruled crosshatching, is the antithesis of what he saw as Whistler's "feast of facile and dainty sketching on copper."[4] Sickert rejected the *préciosité* of Whistler, believing that the "Master" suffered from "an overdose of taste."[5] He handed his plates over to a commercial printer to be "printed like visiting cards" to escape from the fetish of *la belle épreuve*.

1 Sickert to Alfred Pollard, 19 May 1879, quoted by Getscher, *The Stamp of Whistler*, p. 206, and discovered by Wendy Baron.

2 Robert Emmons, *The Life and Opinions of Walter Sickert* London: Faber and Faber, 1941, p. 32, quoted by Getscher, *Stamp*, p. 206.

3 Pennell, *Life*, vol. 2, p. 189.

4 Sickert, "Round and About Whistler", in *A Free House!*, p. 11. Sickert's ideas about etching are discussed in this essay.

5 Sickert, "Round and About Whistler", p. 22.

62   Charles Henry White
Canadian (1878-1918)
Long Dock, Baltimore 1908
First state
Etching and drypoint with plate tone printed in
dark brown ink on cream wove paper
12.3 x 20.1 cm (imp.)
Gift of Touche Ross, 1979
Acc. no. 79/205

63   John William Joseph Winkler
American (b. 1894)
Shipping 1919
Etching in warm black ink on Japanese paper
14.3 x 18.7 cm (imp.)
Signed in pencil below plate right "Winkler"
Gift of the Canadian National Exhibition
Association, 1966
Acc. no. 121

Charles Henry White was born in Hamilton, Ontario, Canada, on 14 April 1878. Although his descendents still live there, no information appears to be available about his life in this country. He was educated partly in the United States and partly in Europe. He studied for a time at the Art Students' League in New York City, then went to Europe in 1901 and spent time at the Académie Laurens and the Académie Constant, Paris.[1] In 1901 he met Joseph Pennell in Venice, who introduced him to the art of etching. Upon his return to the United States in 1901, he made views of a number of major American cities, among them Baltimore, where Whistler lived during the spring and summer of 1855, and the only American city he ever claimed as a birthplace.

It is not known whether Baltimore held a special interest for White on account of the Whistler connection, although White did consider himself to be a "pupil of Whistler."[2] In *Long Dock, Baltimore* he comes close to Whistler's Thames etchings in subject, and in style to his drypoints of the 1860s.

White returned to Europe in 1909 and continued to make picturesque etched views of cities in Belgium and France, revisiting Venice in 1910. He was a successful etcher, but died young after a protracted illness. A large body of well-organized and annotated proofs was left to his family.

1 I am very grateful to Rosemarie L. Tovell, Assistant Curator in the Department of Prints and Drawings at the National Gallery of Canada, for giving me this information on Charles Henry White. Some years ago, I had the opportunity of looking through White's complete work in Hamilton, Ontario, at the invitation of the artist's grand-daughter.

2 *American Art Annual* 12 (1915): 502.

Born in Vienna in 1894, Winkler decided while still at school to go to America to see the "wild west."[1] After working his way across the continent, he settled in San Francisco. He enrolled at the San Francisco Institute of Art, and began to make etchings around 1912.

Winkler first saw Whistler's prints at the Panama-Pacific Exposition in San Francisco in 1915. His work shows a strong indebtedness to Whistler, especially the Whistler of the French and Thames sets. *Shipping* may have been inspired by Whistler's drypoint of 1867, *Shipping at Liverpool* (K. 94). Winkler uses a similar vantage-point, in which the viewer looks straight onto the deck of the boat, with the masts cut off at the upper margin. The use of a very crisp, clean line, while leaving water and sky virtually unworked, are derived from Whistler's Thames etchings of 1859.

Winkler printed most of his plates in small editions on old paper, and bit many of them in the manner of Whistler's Venice etchings by floating nitric acid on the surface and moving it back and forth.

1 Getscher, in his *The Stamp of Whistler* (p. 280), corrected Winkler's birthdate to 1894 from 1890.

63 Winkler, *Shipping*, 1919

62 White, *Long Dock, Baltimore*, 1908

LIST OF ABBREVIATIONS

Principal *catalogues raisonnés* and collections

A.   Arms, Dorothy Noyes, Probstfield, Marie, and Hayes, May Bradshaw. "The Descriptive Catalogue of the Work of John Taylor Arms." Unpublished MS, 1962. New York Public Library.

BP   Birnie Philip Collection, Glasgow University Library.

C.   Carter, Charles. *Etchings and Drypoints from 1924 by James McBey*. Aberdeen: Aberdeen Art Gallery, 1962.

Ch.   Chesson, W.H. Catalogue in *The Work of Charles Keene*, by Joseph Pennell. London: T. Fisher Unwin and Bradbury, Agnew and Co., 1897.

GUL BP   Glasgow University Library, Birnie Philip Collection.

K.   Kennedy, Edward G. *The Etched Work of Whistler*. 6 vols. New York: Grolier Club, 1910.

L.   Levy, Mervyn. *Whistler Lithographs: An Illustrated Catalogue Raisonné*. London: Jupiter Books, 1975.

LC PC   Library of Congress, Washington, D.C., Pennell Collection.

L.D.   Delteil, Loys. *Le peintre-graveur illustré, XIXe siècle*. 32 vols. Paris: L'auteur, 1906-30.

Lugt   Lugt, Fritz. *Les Marques de collections de dessins et d'estampes*. Amsterdam: Vereenigde Drukkerijen, 1921.

PC LC   Pennell Collection, Library of Congress, Washington, D.C.

S.   Strange, Edward F. *The Etched and Engraved Work of Frank Short*. London: George Allen & Sons, 1908.

Sch.   Schneiderman, Richard S. *A Catalogue Raisonné of the Prints of Sir Francis Seymour Haden*. London: Robin Garton, 1983.

W.   Way, T.R. *The Lithographs by Whistler*. New York: Kennedy and Co., 1914.

W.   Wuerth, Louis A. *Catalogue of the Etchings of Joseph Pennell*. Boston (Mass.): Little, Brown and Co., 1928.

W.   Wuerth, Louis A. *Catalogue of the Lithographs of Joseph Pennell*. Boston (Mass.): Little, Brown and Co., 1931.

Y.   Young, Andrew McLaren, Margaret MacDonald, Robin Spencer, Hamish Miles. The Paintings of James McNeill Whistler. 2 vols. London and Newhaven: Yale University Press, 1980.

Z.   Zigrosser, Carl. *The Complete Etchings of John Marin*. Philadelphia, 1969.

Editor: Robert Stacey
Graphic Design: Richard Male Design Associates
Photography: Photographic Services, Art Gallery of Ontario
Composition: Canadian Composition Inc.
Printing: Bradbury Tamblyn & Boorne Ltd.
Typeset in Sabon Antiqua and printed on Dulcet